Critical
Issues
in
History

The Ancient World to A. D. 400

Critical Issues in History

UNDER THE EDITORIAL DIRECTION OF *RICHARD E. SULLIVAN*

SIX-VOLUME EDITION

1   *The Ancient World to A.D. 400*
THOMAS W. AFRICA, *University of Southern California*

2   *The Middle Ages, 400-1250*
RICHARD E. SULLIVAN, *Michigan State University*

3   *The Eve of the Modern World, 1250-1648*
J. K. SOWARDS, *Wichita State University*

4   *The Early Modern Era, 1648-1770*
JOHN C. RULE, *Ohio State University*

5   *The Age of Revolution, 1770-1870*
DAVID L. DOWD, *University of Kentucky*

6   *War and Totalitarianism, 1870 to the Present*
JOHN L. SNELL, *University of Pennsylvania*

TWO-VOLUME EDITION

VOLUME I   *Ancient Times to 1648*

VOLUME II   *1648 to the Present*

Critical
Issues
in
History

The Ancient World

to A.D. 400

EDITED WITH INTRODUCTIONS BY

THOMAS W. AFRICA

University of Southern California

D. C. HEATH *and Company, Boston*

ILLUSTRATION CREDITS

Cover: Section and plan, the Coliseum; *page 1:* section, the
Coliseum; Jacques-François Blondel, *Architecture Française,* Paris, 1906.

Library of Congress Catalog Card Number: 67-13486
Copyright © 1967 by D. C. Heath and Company
No part of the material covered by this copyright
may be reproduced in any form without written permission
of the publisher.
Printed in the United States of America.

Printed December 1966

Boston
Englewood
Indianapolis
Dallas
San Francisco
Atlanta

PREFACE

This volume, one of a six-volume set, is intended to engage students in *problem-resolving situations* as a technique for enriching their study of European history. The editors who collaborated in preparing these six volumes are convinced that this approach has great value in stimulating interest, encouraging critical thinking, and enhancing historical-mindedness, especially when it is used to supplement the more conventional techniques employed in teaching the general introductory course in European history.

The volume opens with an interpretive essay aimed at placing the five "problems" which follow in the perspective of the period. While all of the problems follow the same structure, the topics they treat are highly diverse: in one, a single man's role in history is debated, while the next examines an ideological issue; in one problem causes are sought, while the next weighs effects.

Each of the five problems is introduced by a short statement defining the issue and directing the student to the crucial questions involved. For the most part selections have been taken from the works of modern historians, with occasional use of the observations of contemporary witnesses. In choosing the selections, the editor has tried to avoid generating conflict for conflict's sake. Rather, he has sought to show how honest divergencies emerge among historians as a result of the complexities of history, varying initial assumptions, different approaches to evidence, and all the other factors that enter into interpretation of the past. The student's efforts to understand how differing interpretations arise and to resolve these differences should increase his ability to manipulate historical data and concepts and deepen his understanding of the historian's craft.

CONTENTS

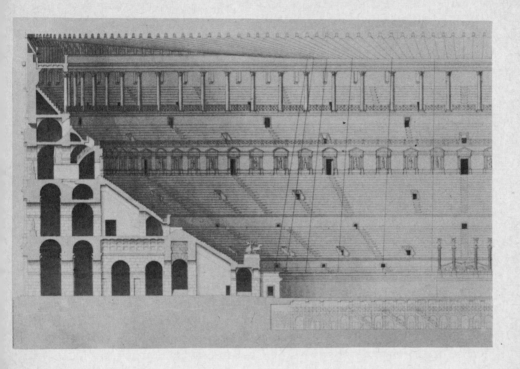

INTRODUCTION

There are many definitions of history, and all are highly personal. "History," said James Joyce, "is a nightmare from which I am trying to awake." Many modern students feel caught in the grip of events and agree with Joyce. History to Napoleon was "the only true philosophy," but he had imagined answers in history where there are usually only questions. The American folk hero, Henry Ford, announced, "History is bunk!" Some students may agree with him, but Henry was not well informed and thought that Benedict Arnold was a novelist. Had he known more about history, Ford might not have been a rabid anti-Semite. Ideally, knowledge of the past adds perspective to our view of the present and our hopes for the future. A sound grasp of history is an essential mark of the sophisticated man. The late John F. Kennedy was a member of the American Historical Association, and Winston Churchill won a Nobel prize for his historical works. Many people, particularly politicians, often claim that "history proves" whatever they are advocating, but it is a difficult matter to know what happened in the past and what it really proves. In the words of Marguerite Yourcenar, "here and there protrude the granite peaks of the inevitable, but all about is rubble from the landslides of chance." The complexity and multiplicity of human events is dazzling, and the historian (like anyone else) is presumptuous when he poses as a prophet. On the other hand, the study of history provides informed opinions on human behavior. Our own experiences are limited, and maturity is a slow and painful process—through history we may observe other men's trials without suffering their agonies. If we can see the world through their eyes, we gain new dimensions as human beings. When we realize that polytheism was the faith of Socrates, our understanding of religion grows. If we can comprehend the horror which reasonable men once felt about witches and ghosts, we may be better able to banish irrational fears from our own minds. To understand himself is the greatest accomplishment of man, and a knowledge of history can aid in this difficult endeavor.

Unlike the mute beasts, man is aware of the past experiences of his species, and this conscious awareness of the past is history. For 5,000 years he has kept a record of his achievements and follies—the record is not always edifying nor even necessarily clear, but it is always interesting and ever pertinent. Since each generation is unique, belief in cycles of history is an occult superstition. Yet, human behavior changes little if at all, and similar problems trouble men in different eras. History is full of useful analogies, but an analogy is not an answer but a stimulus to thought. The first 3,500 years of man's remembered existence is ancient history, a time of great vitality and variety in men and institutions. The ancient world differed from ours in two major respects: men had no inherent rights apart from those derived from society, and production depended on human and animal muscle power. It is true that the peoples of antiquity had outlandish names and believed in gods and notions which we have rejected, but these minor differences should not blind us to the common human denominator in their lives and ours. The development and demise of Athenian democracy and the collapse of the Roman republic are topics of more than academic interest to modern Americans, and life under the Roman Empire sheds considerable light on authoritarian society. The origins of Christianity and Judaism are vital subjects which deserve better treatment than they get in poor novels and worse films. In antiquity, man created civilization for better or worse, and it is imperative that we learn what he did with it and what it did to him.

About 3,000 B.C. history began in the city-states of Mesopotamia and the kingdom of Egypt. To an extent, both societies were managerial states with large educated bureaucracies. In Egypt the god-king preceded the bureaucracy but in Mesopotamia the bureaucrats preceded the kings. In the Near East the advanced societies kept tight controls over the masses and could mobilize great labor forces for irrigation work or the construction of temples, palaces, and pyramids. Trade flourished and with it a commercial mentality and an appreciation of mathematics; the Babylonians devised place-value notation, so dear to the heart of "new math" enthusiasts. In their heyday, the Egyptians had great concern for the afterlife and developed an elaborate funerary cult, but unlike modern Americans, they did not fear death and did not seek to hide it—rather they rejoiced at the prospect of serving the gods forever in paradise. The Mesopotamians took a gloomier view of death and felt that man returned to dust—the first novel of ideas, the Gilgamesh Epic, is based on this pessimistic theme of mortality and futility. In the first millennium B.C. great military empires arose. The grim Assyrians ruled with calculated cruelty and inflicted endless atrocities on their neighbors, but the policy of terror failed to break resistance and the Assyrians only reaped the hatred of their victims. When Assyria fell, the subject peoples "clapped their hands in glee." By the end of the sixth century B.C. the Persians ruled a great empire, stretching from the Balkans to the Indus valley. Cleverer than the Assyrians, the Persians won over their subjects by displaying great respect for local gods and customs. Wealthy, huge, and powerful, the Persian Empire was almost a universal state. The state religion of Persia was Zarathustrianism, which insisted on the immortality and moral accountability of man. To the Zarathustrian priests, the world was a battleground between the forces of darkness and the followers of God. In Palestine the Hebrews had evolved a highly ethical religion and a monotheistic view of God, who naturally was on the side of Israel. Because of the exclusiveness of Judaism, the religion of Israel had little appeal to the pagan world even after the Hebrew scriptures were translated into Greek.

Among moderns, the Greeks are the best known of ancient peoples, but they should not be judged solely by their poets and the Parthenon. Physically, the Hellenes lived in Greece and on the coasts of the Black Sea, Asia Minor, Libya, Sicily, Southern Italy, and Southern France. There was no Hellenic nation and only a vague cultural unity. Politically, the Greeks were fragmented into hundreds of tiny city-states, all fiercely independent and hostile to each other. Some Hellenic cities were ruled by dictators, more by wealthy oligarchies, but a few explored popular government and developed democracy. Athens, in particular, flourished under a highly workable democracy. However, Sparta was a unique totalitarian state devoted to military preparedness, yet reluctant to wage war, for the Spartans always feared that their oppressed serfs might rise against them. The exploitation of man was commonplace in Hellas, and Athens contained great numbers of slaves. The Greeks considered women inferior, stupid, and childlike. The gods cared little for ethics, and Greek religion was often orgiastic. In general, the Greeks were brutal, materialistic, and petty, but they also had a sense of humor and a love of beauty. Some were curious about the nature of man and the universe and laid the foundations of Western thought. Only a few Greeks knew or cared about science or philosophy, but Athens allowed considerable freedom of thought and expression, and no church imposed orthodoxy and hounded heretics. The Greeks were too emotional to be rationalists and too clever to be humble, and their literature abounds in silly ideas and brilliant insights. The variety of Greek thought was one of its most attractive features. The great sophist Protagoras said, "Man is the measure of all things," but Socrates insisted that the good man is the measure, and Plato believed that God is the measure. Despite their subtlety in many matters, the Greeks never realized the futility of war or the need for political unity. The Peloponnesian War between Athens and Sparta was the most famous and bloody of the many conflicts which drained the cities of men and treasure. By the late fourth century B.C., the exhausted cities of Hellas were absorbed into the military empire of Philip of Macedon.

Philip's son Alexander conquered the Persian Empire and founded the Hellenistic world. The Near East succumbed to Hellenic culture and the rule of Macedonian kings who built great nations from the debris of Alexander's empire. The new kings were military despots and living gods. City life and sophistication expanded, and Greek thought took on a cosmopolitan tone. The Ptolemaic kings of Egypt commanded a highly elaborate bureaucracy and subsidized science and learning. At Alexandria a great collection of books was assembled and a major institute of advanced research attracted scholars from many lands. The quality of Hellenistic science may be suggested by the work of two men: Eratosthenes estimated the size of the earth with amazing accuracy, and Aristarchus of Samos offered the hypothesis that the earth and the planets were satellites of the sun. As ideas expanded, cities, buildings, and machines grew larger. The Hellenistic peoples loved colossal statues and enormous equipment; war was fought with large armies and huge moving towers. At Syracuse, the great engineer Archimedes constructed elaborate weapons and defensive cranes which kept an entire Roman army at bay. Big and gaudy, the Hellenistic world was also divided and the kings exhausted each other in dynastic wars. For protection, the city-states of Greece experimented with federal unions but it was too late to provide real security. The Greek economy was unable to accommodate expanding populations, and reformers clamored for the abolition of debts and the redistribution of property. In the anxiety of the age, many men sought solace in the mystery cults of Isis and Serapis. For intellectuals, the Epicureans counseled a life of calm moderation in a cold atomic world, while the Stoics advised a stern acceptance of duty and destiny. The Cynics rejected society and convention and preached an anarchic return to nature. Astrology was the great pseudo-science of the Hellenistic age. When the Romans penetrated the East in the second century B.C., the divided and quarreling Hellenistic nations were easily subdued by the Western power.

Like Topsy, the Roman Empire grew without knowing it. While some wars were deliberate acts of aggression, others were unintended, and many were blunders. There was no consistent pattern of imperialism until the second century B.C. As a city-state, Rome had devised republican institutions which in theory maintained a balance between two executives, a popular legislature, and an aristocratic Senate. In practice, the nobles of the Senate ran the republic for their own benefit. The conquest of Carthage and the Hellenistic East made Rome an imperial power, but the stresses of constant war and running an empire ultimately eroded the republic. Many Roman citizens became landless paupers who resided in the capital and sold their votes for subsistence, but the upper classes enjoyed undreamed-of wealth and commanded hordes of slaves. Fierce political struggles by the nobles for glory and graft led to a series of civil wars in the first century B.C. One able politician, Gaius

Julius Caesar, emerged victorious and established a dictatorship, but he was murdered by his former peers in 44 B.C. Caesar's grandnephew and adopted son, Augustus, seized power in another civil war and founded a military despotism which governed efficiently and had the stability of dynastic succession. For the most part, the emperors of Rome were excellent rulers, and the empire was torn by only one brief civil war during the period 30 B.C. to 235 A.D. The Roman republic had exploited the provinces, but the emperors became increasingly generous toward provincials. The republic had been an Italian monopoly, but some of the most famous emperors came from Spain, Africa, and Syria. The much-publicized Roman Peace was a reality, and the peoples of the Mediterranean world enjoyed considerable prosperity and justice within the limits of an authoritarian regime. However, the Roman army turned against society in 235 A.D. and for a half-century set up and removed emperors at will, while the empire was assaulted by Persians in the East and Germanic barbarians in the North. In 285 A.D. the emperor Diocletian restored order and tried to guarantee stability with totalitarian controls. One of Diocletian's successors, Constantine, was a patron of Christianity, and the once-despised sect became the favored religion of the state. For a century the Roman Empire withstood foreign pressures until the Goths broke through in the late fourth century. In 410 A.D. Rome itself was sacked by barbarians and the Western provinces were soon lost to the invaders. The Eastern provinces became the Byzantine Empire, which had a lively history in the Middle Ages. With all of its faults, the Roman Empire in its heyday had shown that men of varied backgrounds could live together and share power with a minimum of injustice and exploitation.

Our knowledge of the ancient world is pieced together from inscriptions, monuments, coins, a few documents, and a sizable body of historical literature. The major historians of Greece and Rome are available in modern translations and are well worth reading. Any student will profit from contact with the curious and fair-minded Herodotus, the disciplined and gloomy Thucydides, Polybius and his attempts at scientific method, the dramatic and patriotic Livy, the grim and cynical Tacitus, Plutarch and his moralizing and hero worship, and the commonsensical Ammianus Marcellinus. The lesser writers—Xenophon, Sallust, Diodorus Siculus, Josephus, Dio Cassius, and even the *Historia Augusta*—also deserve attention, and the serious student will not neglect the New Testament, Eusebius, and the Hebrew books of Samuel, Kings, Chronicles, and Maccabees.

Not always careful with the facts, the ancient historians wrote with feeling and often with dramatic skill. In reading historians of any period, we must be alert for the biases and preconceptions which may have warped their judgment. We must also be on guard against romanticizing and rhetoric, which can make the most dubious "facts" convincing. When authorities conflict (and they always do), the problem can only be resolved with common sense, and the result will be at best a probability. Because the content of history is often emotional, the student of history should be a realist and a skeptic. When a historian's assertions happen to agree with our own prejudices, we can rarely spot the errors in his argument. A case in point would be the emperor Nero, who is portrayed in Christian tradition and cheap films as a monster of cruelty and vice. Maybe he was, but the saintly emperor Marcus Aurelius was also a persecutor of Christians and watched their torments with contempt. The Roman historians always exaggerated the virtues or villainies of famous men, and the anti-Nero sources are overdone and inconsistent. After he was overthrown, Nero received a "bad press" from writers who courted the favor of his successors. Yet, he had been popular in many parts of the empire, and his grave at Rome was strewn with flowers. Nero was not a model ruler and he did commit crimes, but his image in history is largely the result of fiction and libel. It is difficult to shed preconceived opinions, but the mature student of history must make every effort to do so. Even the devil is entitled to a fair trial, and too many men are condemned by historians on the basis of flimsy and biased evidence. While ancient writers were frankly partisan, modern historians try to be objective but they do not always succeed. It is too tempting to fight the battles of the present in the past and damn dead men who remind us of living ones. Though bias is always a defect, there can sometimes be an advantage in a partisan plea — if his bias is not ours, the writer may shock us into seeing things a little differently. The ultimate yardstick is reason tempered with humility.

1

AKHENATON AND MONOTHEISM

In George Orwell's novel *1984*, individuals who are condemned by the state are simply blotted out of history. Their names are deleted from all records, and all references to their existence are consigned to the flames. A similar fate befell the remarkable pharaoh, Amenhotep IV, who preferred to be called Akhenaton and who upset the religious life of Egypt in the fourteenth century B.C. His religious policies so offended the priests of Egypt that after his death the very name of Amenhotep IV was hacked out of all records and his memory was erased from history. Only the tombs at his holy city of Tell el-Amarna were spared, but they lay neglected until the nineteenth century A.D., when the existence of Akhenaton and his novel ideas were recovered for mankind. Unknown for over three thousand years, the episode of the heretic pharaoh threw unexpected light on the religious development of the Ancient Near East.

Amenhotep IV was one of the pharaohs of the Eighteenth Dynasty when Egypt was a great imperial power. Quite often, imperialism in secular affairs results in henotheism in religious matters: one deity becomes the national god and head of the pantheon. Of the myriad gods of Egypt, the Theban deity Amon-Re was the favored god of the pharaohs who attributed their victories to his intercession. The priests of Amon were rich and pampered, and Amon was considered the king of the gods. What is more, Amon had absorbed the attributes of the sun god Re and the creator god Ptah. As creator of the universe and sustainer of all life, Amon-Re was a universal god, omnipotent, omniscient, and concerned for mankind. However, Amon's supremacy did not endanger the cults of the other gods who also received the pious devotion of the Egyptian masses. In 1379 B.C. the young Amenhotep IV became pharaoh and soon drastically altered the state religion of Egypt. He deposed Amon and persecuted his priests, ignored the other gods, and insisted that the Aton was the supreme deity. Aton was an ancient term for the sun, which was venerated at the city of On (Heliopolis). The pharaoh claimed personal revelations from the Aton, changed his own name to Akhenaton,[1] and insisted that he was Aton's son. Since Thebes was a center of Amon worship, the pharaoh abandoned the capital and built a new city for Aton at Tell el-Amarna. A private world, the holy city was called Akhetaton (Horizon of Aton) and was dedicated to the Aton cult. In Egypt Akhenaton's officers ruthlessly hounded the priests of Amon, but the pharaoh was less concerned with foreign affairs and ignored reports of crises in Asia, where hostile neighbors seized the territories of Egypt's vassals in Syria and Palestine. Lost in his private devotions, Akhenaton allowed the Egyptian empire to crumble while Egypt itself was racked with religious strife. A court cult, the Aton religion had no appeal to the Egyptian masses, and the bigotry of the pharaoh infuriated the priests of the ancient gods. The holy city of Akhetaton became a remote isle of piety in a sea of hatred and discord. Oblivious to everything but the Aton, the pharaoh lost touch with reality.

About 1367 the situation changed. The pharaoh's strong-willed mother Tiy took drastic steps to restore order and save the dynasty. She visited Amarna and forced Akhenaton to accept one of his sons-in-law as co-ruler. Reigning at Thebes, the son-in-law halted the persecution and restored Amon-Re as the state god. Since Akhenaton's wife Nefertiti was devoted to the Aton cult, Tiy separated the pharaoh from his wife. The final years of Akhenaton are obscure, but he was dead by 1362. Though Nefertiti continued to worship the Aton in her palace, the priests of Amon ached for revenge on the hated cult. Another son-in-law of Akhenaton ruled from 1361 to 1352—a weak young man whose name Tutankhamon declared his dependence on Amon. His successor Eye was an adherent of the Aton cult but was overthrown in 1348 by a rough general, Horemheb, who was backed by the priests of Amon. The new regime took a thorough vengeance on the Aton cult and every vestige of the heretical faith was destroyed (except for the Amarna tombs). Contemporaries referred to Akhenaton as "the criminal of Akhetaton," and Amenhotep IV was dropped from the lists of Egyptian kings. The victory of Amon was complete, and the Aton cult and its founder vanished from history.

The bizarre reign of Akhenaton was not the only episode in world history in which a visionary ruler tried to impose his private religious views on a nation. The Babylonian king Nabonidus broke with the priests of the state god Marduk, who retaliated by aiding the Persians to take Babylon and overthrow the royal heretic. The Roman emperor Julian tried vainly to restore paganism as the state cult when the bulk of his subjects were Christians. Despite their sincerity and positions of

---

[1] In many older books, his name appears as Ikhnaton. [Editor's note.]

power, these rulers were failures, for a religion cannot be imposed from the top when it has no inherent appeal for the masses. The conversion of states has always been achieved by worldly princes who moved with the times and not against them. The personal tragedy of Akhenaton was probably heightened by a serious illness. The realistic art at Amarna depicts the pharaoh with a pear-shaped torso, tapering legs, and an unnaturally elongated face. Ironically, the grotesque appearance of Akhenaton became a standard of beauty for the Amarna circle, and his family and courtiers were portrayed with similar features. Though his wife Nefertiti was a strikingly beautiful woman, even she was sometimes shown with the eerie features of her husband. A recent study of the mummy of Akhenaton has suggested that the pharaoh probably suffered from a pituitary lesion which caused his progressive physical and psychological deterioration.[2] If so, the visionary pharaoh was a pathetic monster and in his final years a madman. In some respects, Akhenaton resembles the Florentine reformer Savonarola: Both were ugly, intolerant, god-intoxicated men with a deep sense of personal mission. Both reformers claimed divine inspiration, but the friar at least did not claim to be the son of god.

Whatever the weaknesses of the royal prophet, the Aton religion with its bigoted exclusion of other gods was a close approximation to monotheism. The American Egyptologist, James H. Breasted, deeply admired Akhenaton and insisted that the revolutionary pharaoh was "the first monotheist" and that the Aton doctrine had somehow influenced Hebrew thought. Breasted was a colorful and persuasive writer and his books convinced Freud and many others that Akhenaton was indeed a monotheist and that Mosaic monotheism was related to Atonism. Though still popular among general readers, Breasted's views were challenged by many scholars, and most Egyptologists reject his enthusiastic idealization of the Aton cult and its founder. The personality and beliefs of Moses present a historical problem of great complexity, because of the composite and contradictory nature of the Biblical texts which describe the man and his laws. Since the name Moses is Egyptian and he is associated with the Egyptian custom of circumcision, it is not unlikely that Moses was an Egyptian. The tradition that he was raised at the phar- aoh's court reinforces this conclusion, and even if the tale of the babe in the bulrushes is true, Moses was a highly Egyptianized individual. However, any connection between Moses and Akhenaton is extremely doubtful, for the Exodus took place over a century after the death of the heretic pharaoh. The first and only reference in Egyptian annals to the existence of the Hebrews is an inscription by the pharaoh Merneptah, who boasted that he defeated Israel and other Asiatic tribes about 1232 B.C. If the Israelites were on the borders of Palestine by this date, Moses could not have been a contemporary of Akhenaton. Nor could the great lawgiver have had any knowledge of the Aton religion which had been destroyed root and branch years before. While it is possible that some memories of Atonism were preserved by the priests at On, there was an equally rich source of religious thought in the worship of Amon-Re, the all-powerful lord of the universe and father

---

[2] Cyril Aldred and A. T. Sandison, "The Pharaoh Akhenaten: A Problem in Egyptology and Pathology," *Bulletin of the History of Medicine* (1962), Vol. 36, 293–316.

of mankind. As one of the pharaoh's courtiers, Moses was surely familiar with the hymns to Amon-Re.

Moreover, the intolerant exclusiveness of the Aton cult with its hatred of other gods was not characteristic of early Hebrew religion, which accepted the existence of other national deities.[3] While Moses was on Sinai communing with Yahweh, his followers were dancing before a golden bull, and Solomon, "the Lord's anointed," later worshiped the gods of his many wives. The Israelites had great difficulty shaking free from an anthropomorphic concept of Yahweh. Only gradually did the religion of Israel evolve into a true monotheism. This momentous step in the history of religion took centuries to achieve and was the work of the great prophets who agonized over the nature of their national god and devised the premises of Judaism. Hebrew monotheism was a product of the tribulations of Israel and the intellects of the prophets—it was not a hollow echo of the bizarre cult of a fanatic pharaoh who had been swallowed by the mists of time.

[3] The author of II Kings 3:26–27 attributes the victory of the Moabites to the power of their god Chemosh. [Editor's note.]

TWO RIVAL HYMNS

1. A HYMN TO AMON-RE

The imperial god of Egypt, Amon-Re, was a blend of the Theban deity Amon and the sun god Re. To his worshipers, Amon-Re was "chief of all gods, the good god, the beloved, who gives life to all that is warm." The following hymn was composed before the reign of Akhenaton and celebrates Amon as the sun, as the creator, and as the protector of mankind.

The sweetness of thee is in the northern sky.
The beauty of thee carries away hearts;
The love of thee makes arms languid;
Thy beautiful form relaxes the hands;
And hearts are forgetful at the sight of thee.
Thou art the sole one, who made all that is,
The solitary sole one, who made what exists,
From whose eyes mankind came forth,
And upon whose mouth the gods came into being.
He who made herbage for the cattle,
And the fruit tree for mankind,
Who made that on which the fish in the river may live,
And the birds soaring in the sky.
He who gives breath to that which is in the egg,
Gives life to the son of the slug,
And makes that on which gnats may live,

From *Ancient Near Eastern Texts Relating to the Old Testament,* ed. James B. Pritchard, 2nd ed. (Princeton, 1955), pp. 366–67. Reprinted by permission of the Princeton University Press. Copyright © 1955 by the Princeton University Press. Translated by John A. Wilson.

And worms and flies in like manner;
Who supplies the needs of the mice in their holes,
And gives life to flying things in every tree.
Hail to thee, who did all this!
Solitary sole one, with many hands,
Who spends the night wakeful, while all men are asleep,
Seeking benefit for his creatures.
Amon, enduring in all things, . . .
Praises are thine, when they all say:
"Jubilation to thee, because thou weariest thyself with us!
Salaams to thee, because thou didst create us!"
Hail to thee for all beasts!
Jubilation to thee for every foreign country—
To the height of heaven, to the width of earth,
To the depth of the great green sea!
The gods are bowing down to thy majesty
And exalting the might of him who created them,
Rejoicing at the approach of him who begot them.
They say to thee: "Welcome in peace!
Father of the fathers of all the gods,
Who raised the heavens and laid down the ground,
Who made what is and created what exists;
Sovereign—life, prosperity, health!—and chief of the gods!
We praise thy might, according as thou didst make us.
Let us act for thee, because thou brought us forth.
We give thee thanksgiving because thou hast wearied thyself with us!"
Hail to thee, who made all that is!
Lord of truth and father of the gods,
Who made mortals and created beasts,
Lord of the grain,
Who made also the living of the beasts of the desert.
Amon, the bull beautiful of countenance,
The beloved in Karnak, ...
The horizon-dweller, Horus of the east,
From whom the desert creates silver and gold,
Genuine lapis lazuli for love of him.

A HYMN TO THE ATON

The most impressive of the Aton hymns was found in the tomb of Eye at Tell el-Amarna. Admirers of Akhenaton have seen a connection between this hymn and the 104th Psalm. The Aton hymn differs from the Amon-Re hymn, not in religious intensity or intellectual scope, but in slighting the other gods and celebrating the prophet Akhenaton.

From *Ancient Near Eastern Texts Relating to the Old Testament*, ed. James B. Pritchard, 2nd ed. (Princeton, 1955), pp. 370–71. Reprinted by permission of the Princeton University Press. Copyright © 1955 by the Princeton University Press. Translated by John A. Wilson.

Thou appearest beautifully on the horizon of heaven,
Thou living Aton, the beginning of life!
When thou art risen on the eastern horizon,
Thou hast filled every land with thy beauty.
Thou art gracious, great, glistening, and high over every land;
Thy rays encompass the lands to the limit of all that thou hast made:
As thou art Re, thou reachest to the end of them;
Thou subduest them for thy beloved son.
Though thou art far away, thy rays are on earth;
Though thou art in their faces, no one knows thy going.
When thou settest in the western horizon,
The land is in darkness, in the manner of death. . . .
At daybreak, when thou arisest on the horizon,
When thou shinest as the Aton by day,
Thou drivest away the darkness and givest thy rays.
The Two Lands are in festivity every day,
Awake and standing upon their feet,
For thou hast raised them up.
Washing their bodies, taking their clothing,
Their arms are raised in praise at thy appearance.
All the world, they do their work.
All beasts are content with their pasturage;
Trees and plants are flourishing.
The birds which fly from their nests,
Their wings are stretched out in praise to [thee,]
All beasts spring upon their feet.
Whatever flies and alights,
They live when thou hast risen for them.
The ships are sailing north and south as well,
For every way is open at thy appearance.
The fish in the river dart before thy face;
Thy rays are in the midst of the great green sea.
Creator of seed in women,
Thou who makest fluid into man,
Who maintainest the son in the womb of his mother,
Who soothest him with that which stills his weeping,
Thou nurse even in the womb,
Who givest breath to sustain all that he has made!
When he descends from the womb to breathe
On the day when he is born,
Thou openest his mouth completely,
Thou suppliest his necessities.
When the chick in the egg speaks within the shell,
Thou givest him breath within it to maintain him. . . .
How manifold it is, what thou hast made!
They are hidden from the face of man.
O sole god, like whom there is no other!
Thou didst create the world according to thy desire,
Whilst thou wert alone:
All men, cattle, and wild beasts,
Whatever is on earth, going upon its feet,
And what is on high, flying with its wings.
The countries of Syria and Nubia, the land of Egypt,

A Hymn to the Aton

Thou settest every man in his place,
Thou suppliest their necessities:
Everyone has his food, and his time of life is reckoned.
Their tongues are separate in speech,
And their natures as well;
Their skins are distinguished,
As thou distinguishest the foreign peoples.
Thou makest a Nile in the underworld,
Thou bringest it forth as thou desirest
To maintain the people of Egypt
According as thou madest them for thyself,
The lord of all of them, wearying himself with them,
The lord of every land, rising for them,
The Aton of the day, great of majesty.
All distant foreign countries, thou makest their life also,
For thou hast set a Nile in heaven,
That it may descend for them and make waves upon the mountains,
Like the great green sea,
To water their fields in their towns.
How effective they are, thy plans, O lord of eternity!
The Nile in heaven, it is for the foreign peoples
And for the beasts of every desert that go upon their feet;
While the true Nile comes from the underworld for Egypt.
Thy rays suckle every meadow.
When thou risest, they live, they grow for thee.
Thou makest the seasons in order to rear all that thou hast made,
The winter to cool them,
And the heat that they may taste thee.
Thou hast made the distant sky in order to rise therein,
In order to see all that thou dost make.
Whilst thou wert alone,
Rising in thy form as the living Aton,
Appearing, shining, withdrawing or approaching,
Thou madest millions of forms of thyself alone.
Cities, towns, fields, road, and river—
Every eye beholds thee over against them,
For thou art the Aton of the day over the earth. . . .
Thou art in my heart,
And there is no other that knows thee
Save thy son [Akhenaton,]
For thou hast made him well-versed in thy plans and in thy strength. . . .
All work is laid aside when thou settest in the west.
But when thou risest again,
Everything is made to flourish for the king, . . .
Since thou didst found the earth
And raise them up for thy son,
Who came forth from thy body:
The King of Upper and Lower Egypt, . . . Akhenaton, . . . and the Chief Wife of the
King . . . Nefertiti, living and youthful forever and ever.

JAMES H. BREASTED

AKHENATON: "THE FIRST INDIVIDUAL"

James H. Breasted (1865 – 1935) of the University of Chicago was a pioneer American Egyptologist. His doctoral dissertation (Berlin, 1894) dealt with Akhenaton.
Learned, tireless, and enthusiastic, he was a popular speaker and a prolific writer.
His lively books—*A History of Egypt* (1905), *Development of Religion and Thought
in Ancient Egypt* (1912), *Ancient Times* (1916), *The Conquest of Civilization*
(1926), and *The Dawn of Conscience* (1933)—were widely read, and his view of
Akhenaton reached a large public. Originally, Breasted aspired to the ministry and
his religious leanings are apparent in his interpretation of Akhenaton, the "first
monotheist."

Amenhotep IV immersed himself heart and soul
in the thought of the time, and the philosophizing
theology of the priests was of more importance to
him than all the provinces of Asia. In such con-
templations he gradually developed ideals and purposes which make him the most remarkable of all
the Pharaohs, and, we may even say, the first
individual in human history. . . . It was universalism
expressed in terms of imperial power which first
caught the imagination of the thinking men of the
empire, and disclosed to them the universal sweep
of the Sun-god's dominion as a physical fact. In the
Ancient East monotheism was but imperialism in
religion. Already under Amenhotep III an old name
for the material sun, "Aton," had come into prominent use, where the name of the Sun-god might have
been expected. . . . A cult of the newly named Sun-
god had . . . been inaugurated and . . . he had
even been designated as "the sole god" by Amenhotep III's contemporaries. Amenhotep IV was soon
closely associated with the new ideas. . . . Early
in his reign we find him . . . engaged in the worship
of Aton . . . but . . . it was not merely Sun-
worship. . . . The king was evidently deifying the
light or the vital heat which he found accompanying
all life. . . .

Amenhotep IV possessed unlimited personal force
of character, and he was moreover the son of a line
of rulers too strong and too illustrious to be . . . set
aside, even by the most powerful priesthood in the
land. A bitter conflict ensued, in which the issue
was sharply drawn between Aton and the old gods.
It rendered Thebes intolerable to the young king.
He decided to break with the priesthoods and to
make Aton the sole god, not merely in his own
thought, but in very fact. As far as their external and
material manifestations and equipment were concerned, the annihilation of the old gods could be and
was accomplished without delay. The priesthoods,
including that of Amon, were dispossessed, the official temple-worship of the various gods throughout
the land ceased, and their names were erased where-
ever they could be found upon the monuments.
The persecution of Amon was especially severe.
The cemetery of Thebes was visited and in the
tombs of the ancestors the hated name of Amon was
hammered out wherever it appeared upon the
stone. . . . The royal statues of his ancestors,
including even the king's father, were not respected,
and . . . the young king was . . . obliged to cut
out his own father's name in order to prevent
the name of Amon from appearing. . . . The king's
own name, likewise Amenhotep, . . . was of
necessity also banished and the king assumed in
its place the name "Ikhnaton," which means
"Aton is satisfied." . . .

This terrible revolution, violating all that was dearest
and most sacred in Egyptian life, must have been a

From James H. Breasted, "Ikhnaton, the Religious Revolutionary," *The Cambridge Ancient History* (Cambridge, Eng., 1926), Vol. II,
pp. 109–17, 119–21, 125–28. Reprinted by permission of the Cambridge University Press.

devastating experience for the youthful king, perhaps not yet nineteen at this time. Thebes had become an impossible place of residence. . . . In the sixth year of his reign and shortly after he had changed his name, the king was living in his own Aton-city in Egypt. He chose as its site a fine and spacious bay in the cliffs . . . nearly three hundred miles below Thebes. He called it Akhetaton, "Horizon of Aton"—it is known in modern times as Tell el-Amarna. . . . All that was devised and done in the new city and in the propagation of the Aton faith bears the stamp of Ikhnaton's individuality. . . . The men about him, in spite of his youth, must have been irresistibly swayed by the young Pharaoh's unbending will. But Ikhnaton understood enough of the old policy of the Pharaohs to know that he must hold his party by practical rewards, and the leading partisans of his movement . . . enjoyed liberal bounty at his hands. . . . Although there must have been a nucleus of men who really appreciated the ideal aspects of the king's teaching, . . . many were not uninfluenced by "the loaves and the fishes." . . .

Of all the monuments left by this unparalleled revolution, the Aton hymns are by far the most remarkable; and . . . Psalm 104 shows a notable similarity to [one Aton] hymn both in the thought and the sequence. . . . In this great hymn the universalism of the empire finds full expression and the royal singer sweeps his eye from the far-off cataracts of the Nubian Nile to the remotest lands of Syria. It is clear that he is projecting a world religion. . . . He bases the universal sway of God upon his fatherly care of all men alike, irrespective of race or nationality. . . . Ikhnaton thus grasped the idea of a world-lord, as the creator of nature; but the king likewise saw revealed the creator's beneficent purpose for all his creatures, even the meanest. He discerned in some measure the goodness of the All-Father as did He who bade us consider the lilies. . . .

Our sources do not show us that the king had perceptibly risen from a discernment of the beneficence to a conception of the righteousness in the character of God, nor for His demand for this in the character of men. Nevertheless, there is in Ikhnaton's "teaching" . . . a constant emphasis upon "truth" such as is not found before or since. . . . He had himself depicted on the monuments while enjoying the most familiar and unaffected intercourse with

his family. . . . The art of the age was unavoidably affected by this extraordinary revolution, and . . . the king's person . . . was no exception to the law of the new art; the artists represented Ikhnaton as they *saw* him. . . .

Wholly absorbed in the exalted religion to which he had given his life, stemming the tide of tradition . . . , this young revolutionary of twenty-five was beset with too many enterprises and responsibilities of a totally different nature to give much attention to the affairs of the empire abroad. . . . Both in Syria and Palestine the provinces of the Pharaoh had gradually passed entirely out of Egyptian control, and . . . the Egyptian empire in Asia was for the time at an end. At Akhetaton, the new and beautiful capital, the splendid temple of Aton resounded with hymns to the new god of the empire, while the empire itself was no more. . . . The storm which had broken over his Asiatic empire was not more disastrous than that which threatened the fortunes of his house in Egypt. But he was steadfast as before in the propagation of his new faith. At his command temples of Aton had now arisen all over the land. He devoted himself to the elaboration of the temple ritual and the tendency to theologize somewhat dimmed the earlier freshness of the hymns to the god.

Meanwhile, the national convulsion which his revolution had precipitated was producing the most disastrous consequences throughout the land. The Aton faith disregarded some of the most cherished beliefs of the people, especially those regarding the hereafter. Osiris, their old time protector and friend in the world of darkness, was banished from the tomb, and the magical paraphernalia which was to protect them from a thousand foes was gone. . . . The Aton faith remained but the cherished theory of the idealist, Ikhnaton, and a little court-circle; it never really became the religion of the people. Added to the secret resentment and opposition of the people, we must consider also far more dangerous forces. During all of Ikhnaton's reign a powerful priestly party, openly or secretly, did all in its power to undermine him. Among the army and its leaders, the neglect and loss of the Asiatic empire must have turned against the king many a strong man. . . . Ikhnaton might appoint one of his favorites to the command of the army, but his ideal aims and his high motives for peace would be as unpopular as they were unintelligible to his commanders. . . . Thus, both the people and the priestly and military classes alike were fomenting plans to overthrow the hated dreamer in the palace of the Pharaohs, of whose thoughts they understood so little. To increase Ikhnaton's danger, fortune had decreed him no son, and he was obliged to depend for support, as the years passed, upon his son-in-law, a noble named Sakere. . . . Ikhnaton had probably never been physically strong; his spare face, with the lines of an ascetic, shows increasing traces of the cares which weighed so heavily upon him. He finally nominated Sakere as his successor and appointed him at the same time co-regent. He survived but a short time after this, and about 1358 B.C., having reached his seventeenth regnal year, he succumbed to the overwhelming forces that were against him. . . .

Thus disappeared the most remarkable figure in earlier oriental history. The sumptuous inscriptions on his beautiful coffin . . . call him "the living Aton's beautiful child who lives forever and is true (or just, or righteous) in sky and earth." To his own nation he was afterwards known as "the criminal of Akhetaton"; but however much we may censure him for the loss of the empire, which he allowed to slip from his fingers, however much we may condemn the fanaticism with which he pursued his aim, even to the violation of his own father's name and monuments, there died with him such a spirit as the world had never seen before—a brave soul, undauntedly facing the momentum of immemorial tradition, and thereby stepping out from the long line of conventional and colorless Pharaohs, that he might disseminate ideas far beyond and above the capacity of his age to understand. Among the Hebrews, seven or eight hundred years later, we look for such men; but the modern world has yet adequately to value or even acquaint itself with this man, who, in an age so remote and under conditions so adverse, became not only the world's first idealist and the world's first *individual*, but also the earliest monotheist, and the first prophet of internationalism—the most remarkable figure of the Ancient World before the Hebrews.

SIGMUND FREUD

MOSES AND THE ATON CULT

The founder of psychoanalysis, Sigmund Freud (1856–1939), was a man of wide interests with a particular fondness for Egyptology and antiquity. The figure of Moses attracted him, and Freud identified himself with the great liberator and lawgiver of Hebrew tradition. Despite his towering stature in psychology, Freud was not a historian and his version of Moses and the Aton cult was based on an uncritical acceptance of the theories of Breasted and a German scholar, Ernst Sellin. Aware that his interpretation of history was shaky at best, Freud admitted: "It is enough that I myself can believe in the solution to the problem. It has pursued me through my whole life." After publishing two articles on Moses in the psychoanalytical journal *Imago* in 1937, Freud returned to the topic in his final work, *Moses and Monotheism* (1939).

To deny a people the man whom it praises as the greatest of its sons is not a deed to be undertaken light-heartedly—especially by one belonging to that people. No consideration, however, will move me to set aside truth in favor of supposed national interests. . . .

The man Moses, the liberator of his people, who

gave them their religion and their laws, belonged to an age so remote that the preliminary question arises whether he was a historical person or a legendary figure. If he lived, his time was the thirteenth or fourteenth century B.C.; we have no word of him except from the Holy Books and the written traditions of the Jews. Although the decision lacks final historical certainty, the great majority of historians have expressed the opinion that Moses did live and that the exodus from Egypt, led by him, did in fact take place. It has been maintained with good reason that the later history of Israel could not be understood if this were not admitted. . . . The suggestion has long been made and by many different people that the name Moses derives from the Egyptian vocabulary. Instead of citing all the authors who have voiced this opinion, I shall quote a passage from a recent work by Breasted, an author whose *History of Egypt* is regarded as authoritative: "It is important to notice that his name, Moses, was Egyptian. It is simply the Egyptian word 'mose' meaning 'child,' and is an abridgement of a fuller form of such names as 'Amen-mose' . . . or 'Ptah-mose'. . . ." I have given this passage literally and am by no means prepared to share the responsibility for its details. I am a little surprised, however, that Breasted in citing related names should have passed over the analogous theophorous names in the list of Egyptian kings, such as Ah-mose, Thut-mose . . ., and Ra-mose. . . .

It might have been expected that one of the many authors who recognized Moses to be an Egyptian name would have drawn the conclusion, or at least considered the possibility, that the bearer of an Egyptian name was himself an Egyptian. . . . We are not at all surprised to find that the poet Chamisso was of French extraction, Napoleon Buonaparte, on the other hand, of Italian, and that Benjamin Disraeli was an Italian Jew, as his name would lead us to expect[1]. . . . Nevertheless, to the best of my knowledge no historian has drawn this conclusion in the case of Moses, not even one of those who, like Breasted, are ready to suppose that Moses "was cognizant of all the wisdom of the Egyptians." What hindered them from doing so can only be guessed at. Perhaps the awe of Biblical tradition was insuperable. Perhaps it seemed mon-

[1] It should be noted, however, that Jews from Zerubbabel to Goldberg have often adopted the names of a host culture. [Editor's note.]

strous to imagine that the man Moses could have been anything other than a Hebrew. . . .

[*Freud discusses the legends of early heroes—Romulus and Remus, Sargon of Agade—who were cast adrift as babies in basket-boats. Such tales usually include the claim that the infant is of royal birth and thus justify his later rise to power from humble beginnings.*] . . . It is very different in the case of Moses. Here the first family—usually so distinguished—is modest enough. He is the child of Jewish Levites. But the second family—the humble one in which as a rule heroes are brought up—is replaced by the royal house of Egypt; the princess brings him up as her own son. . . . One of the families is the real one, the one into which the great man was really born and in which he was brought up. The other is fictitious, invented by the myth in pursuance of its own motives. As a rule the real family corresponds with the humble one, the noble family with the fictitious one. In the case of Moses something seemed to be different. And here the new point of view may perhaps bring some illumination. It is that the first family, the one from which the babe is exposed to danger, . . . is in all comparable cases the fictitious one; the second family, however, by which the hero is adopted and in which he grows up, is his real one. If we have the courage to accept this statement as a general truth to which the Moses legend also is subject, then we suddenly see our way clear. Moses is an Egyptian —probably of noble origin—whom the myth undertakes to transform into a Jew. . . . The divergence of the Moses legend from all others of its kind might be traced back to a special feature in the story of Moses' life. Whereas in all other cases the hero rises above his humble beginnings as his life progresses, the heroic life of the man Moses began by descending from his eminence to the level of the children of Israel. . . . But what could have induced a distinguished Egyptian—perhaps a prince, priest, or high official—to place himself at the head of a throng of culturally inferior immigrants and to leave the country with them, is not easy to conjecture. The well-known contempt of the Egyptians for foreigners makes such a proceeding especially unlikely. . . .

The Jewish people in Egypt were certainly not without some kind of religion, and if Moses, who gave them a new religion, was an Egyptian, then the surmise cannot be rejected that this other new religion was the Egyptian one. This possibility encounters an obstacle: the sharp contrast between the Jewish religion attributed to Moses and the Egyptian one. The former is a grandiosely rigid monotheism. . . . In the Egyptian religion, on the other hand, there is a bewildering mass of deities of differing importance and provenance. . . . A strange fact in the history of the Egyptian religion, which was recognized and appraised relatively late, opens up another point of view. It is still possible that the religion Moses gave to his Jewish people was yet his own, *an* Egyptian religion though not *the* Egyptian one. . . . If Moses was an Egyptian and if he transmitted to the Jews his own religion, then it was that of Ikhnaton, the Aton religion. . . . If Moses gave the Jews not only a new religion, but also the law of circumcision, he was no Jew but an Egyptian, and then the Mosaic religion was probably an Egyptian one: namely— because of its contrast to the popular religion—that of Aton, with which the Jewish one shows agreement in some remarkable points. . . . Let us assume that Moses was a noble and distinguished man, perhaps indeed a member of the royal house, as the myth has it. He must have been conscious of his great abilities, ambitious, and energetic; perhaps he saw himself in a dim future as the leader of his people, the governor of the Empire. In close contact with Pharaoh, he was a convinced adherent of the new religion, whose basic principles he fully understood and had made his own. With the king's death and the subsequent reaction, he saw all his hopes and prospects destroyed. If he was not to recant the convictions so dear to him, then Egypt had no more to give him; he had lost his native country. In this hour of need he found an unusual solution. The dreamer Ikhnaton had estranged himself from his people, had let his world empire crumble. Moses' active nature conceived the plan of founding a new empire, of finding a new people, to whom he could give the religion that Egypt disdained. . . . Perhaps he was at the time governor of that border province (Gosen) in which—perhaps already in the "Hyksos period"— certain Semitic tribes had settled. These he chose to be his new people. . . . He established relations with them, placed himself at their head, and directed the Exodus "by strength of hand." In full contradistinction to the Biblical tradition we may suppose this Exodus to have passed off peacefully and without pursuit. The authority of Moses made it possible, and there was then no central power that could have prevented it. . . .

The kernel of our thesis, the dependence of Jewish monotheism on the monotheistic episode in Egyptian history, has been guessed and hinted at by several workers. I need not cite them here, since none of them has been able to say by what means this influence was exerted. Even if, as I suggest, it is bound up with the individuality of Moses, we shall have to weigh other possibilities. . . . It is not to be supposed that the overthrow of the official Aton religion completely put an end to the monotheistic trend in Egypt. The School of Priests at On, from which it emanated, survived the catastrophe and might have drawn whole generations after Ikhnaton into the orbit of their religious thought. That Moses performed the deed is quite thinkable, therefore, even if he did not live in Ikhnaton's time and had not come under his personal influence, even if he were simply an adherent or merely a member of the school of On. This conjecture would postpone the date of the Exodus and bring it nearer to the time usually assumed, the thirteenth century B.C. . . .

In 1922 Ernst Sellin made a discovery of decisive importance. He found in the book of the Prophet Hosea (second half of the eighth century) unmistakable traces of a tradition to the effect that the founder of their religion, Moses, met a violent end in a rebellion of his stubborn and refractory people. The religion he had instituted was at the same time abandoned. . . . Naturally, I am not in a position to decide whether Sellin has correctly interpreted the relevant passages in the Prophets. If he is right, however, we may regard as historically credible the tradition he recognized; for such things are not readily invented—there is no tangible motive for doing so. And if they have really happened, the wish to forget them is easily understood. . . . Among all the events of Jewish prehistory that poets, priests, and historians of a later age undertook to portray, there was an outstanding one the suppression of which was called for by the most obvious and best of human motives. It was the murder of the great leader and liberator Moses, which Sellin divined from clues furnished by the Prophets. Sellin's presumption cannot be called fanciful; it is probable enough. Moses, trained in Ikhnaton's school, employed the same methods as the king; he gave commands and forced his religion on the people. Perhaps Moses' doctrine was still more uncompromising than that of his master; he had no need to retain any connection with the religion of the sun-god since the school of On would have no importance for his alien people. Moses met with the same fate as Ikhnaton, the fate that awaits all enlightened despots. The Jewish people of Moses were quite as unable to bear such a highly spiritualized religion . . . as were the Egyptians of the Eighteenth Dynasty. In both cases the same thing happened: those who felt themselves in tutelage, or who felt dispossessed, revolted and threw off the burden of a religion that had been forced on them. But while the tame Egyptians waited until fate had removed the sacred person of their Pharaoh, the savage Semites took their destiny into their own hands and did away with their tyrant. Nor can we maintain that the Biblical text preserved to us does not prepare us for such an end to Moses. The account of the "wandering in the wilderness"—which might stand for the time of Moses' rule—describes a series of grave revolts against his authority which, by Jahve's command, were suppressed with savage chastisement. It is easy to imagine that one of those revolts came to another end than the text admits.

HARRY R. HALL

AKHENATON: "THE FIRST DOCTRINAIRE"

Not all Egyptologists shared Breasted's enthusiasm for Akhenaton, but few were as caustic as Harry R. Hall (1873–1930), whose *The Ancient History of the Near East* (1913) enjoyed great popularity among British readers. As Keeper of the Department of Egyptian and Assyrian Antiquities, British Museum, Hall was a recognized authority on the ancient Near East. Though he did not admire Akhenaton, Hall accepted Breasted's notion that the heretical Pharaoh had been a monotheist. In the following passages, Hall falls into errors of his own, namely nineteenth-century racism.

The son of Amenhetep III and Tii was no Egyptian warrior like his ancestors. Of mixed race, with, probably, the alien blood of Aryan Mitanni inherited from his father and of the wild desert tribes . . . derived from his mother running in his veins as well as the ichor of the descendants of Ra, the son of a luxurious and art-loving father and of a clever and energetic mother, he was brought up under strong feminine influence. All the requisites for the creation of a striking and abnormal character were present. Amenhetep IV was a man of entirely original brain, untrammelled on account of his position by those salutary checks which the necessity of mixing with and agreeing with other men of lesser mental calibre imposes on those not born in the purple. His genius had full play. And the result was disaster. So insensate, so disastrous, was his obliviousness to everything else but his own "fads" in religion and art that we can well wonder if Amenhetep IV was not really half insane. Certainly his genius was closely akin to madness. Dithyrambs have been penned, especially in late years, in praise of this philosophic and artistic reformer, "the first individual in ancient history." We might point out that others have an equal right to this characterization, for instance [Hammurabi], Hatshepsut, or [Thutmose III]. . . . Certainly Akhenaten was the first doctrinaire in history, and, what is much the same thing, the first prig.

His religious heresy, the central fact of his reign, was not altogether his own idea. The veneration of the Aten, the disk of the sun, had been growing in court favor during his father's last years. Both Amenhetep III and Tii venerated the Aten as well as Amen-Ra and the other gods. Amenhetep III, as the son prob-

From Harry R. Hall, *The Ancient History of the Near East,* 11 ed. (London, 1950), pp. 298–99, 301–03, 304–08. Reprinted by permission of Methuen & Co., Ltd.

ably of a Mitannian mother, was half an Iranian and may well have felt drawn towards a cult which resembled not remotely Iranian religion. But at the same time he gives us (also an Iranian trait) the impression of a tolerant and easy-going prince, and even if he believed privately that the Aten was the one real god, he would be the last to make enemies of the priests and plunge his country into civil war by publicly announcing his belief. His son was of a different spirit. The feminine cast of his character showed itself at once in a reckless doctrinaire proclamation of a belief which could only be anathema to his less clever subjects, of an adhesion to a "principle" which admitted of no compromise even if it brought his kingdom about his ears and plunged the world in war, which it did. His reign lasted in all not more than eighteen years. . . . Much of the extravagance that followed would probably have been avoided had his father lived longer and been able to keep him in check. The influence of Tii, which must have been paramount during the first years of his reign, when she apparently acted as regent, can hardly have been wisely exercised.

At first the young Amenhetep IV was represented on the monuments in the conventional style of his forefathers. His real peculiarities of body (which was as strangely constituted as his brain) were ignored. Amen and the other gods are still officially worshipped by him five years after his father's death and his accession. In the thirteenth year of his age, probably, he was married to his sister Nefertiti, who evidently sympathized entirely with his ideas. Then came emancipation. In the sixth year of his reign, when he was presumably fifteen years old and therefore fully a man in Egypt, he openly proclaimed his heresy, and the religious revolution was begun. . . . The result was curious. The difficulty of governing Thebes must have been enormous, and it may well be that the king was not safe from assassination there. He therefore combined discretion with valor by ostentatiously shaking the dust of Thebes from off his shoes and proceeding to a new capital which should be free of Amen and his devotees. He would worship his god in his own way, and his court, as was fitting, should worship him too, in his way, in a spot uncontaminated by the previous presence of the absurd superstitions of his unenlightened ancestors. In a desert place, where the unregenerate did not exist, he would found a city called "Akhetaten," . . . where he could teach his "doctrine" to willing hearers only. . . .

We can imagine the effect of these proceedings upon his people: the fury of the priests of Amen; the bitterness of the soldiers and statesmen who saw the work of a dynasty abandoned and thrown aside at the caprice of a boy; the amazement of the Asiatics at the news that the young [Pharaoh] had gone suddenly mad and had vowed never to stir out of his city for the defence of his empire; the resentment of the mass of the Egyptians, soon to crystallize into active hatred of the "criminal of Akhetaten." Yet no overt resistance was possible. The whole machinery of the state was in the king's hands, and his behests were obeyed by the royal officers, probably many of them convinced adherents of the "doctrine." The king's religion was for the moment the religion of the empire, and Amen was deposed from his imperial throne to make way for the Aten. The whole of the property of Amen was simply transferred to the new god, and the Theban priests were driven out or proscribed. . . . Yet a king cannot abolish a national religion by decree, although he may obliterate the names of its gods from their temples, and this fact must soon have been learnt by Akhenaten. We do not know the details of the story, but for the last few years of his reign Thebes must have been in more or less open revolt, no doubt under the leadership of Amen's high-priest, whom the king did not recognize as existing. . . .

Foiled by the dispossessed priests of Amen in his attempt to abolish them and their god utterly, the king finally abandoned his empire to go its own way while he lived his own life with his family and court in the city which he had created. Many of his courtiers no doubt really believed in the new religion, but others, as we see from the readiness with which they abandoned it after his death, never really believed in it, but only conformed to it because it was the king's religion. . . . In the relief of Tell el-Amarna, . . . we see the king represented in what must be almost a caricature of his facial and bodily peculiarities. Probably he liked these peculiarities to be so exaggerated; his already long nose and chin to be made longer, his belly to be represented as pendulous, his legs as bowed. . . . Many of the courtiers . . . show in the reliefs a decided approximation to the same degenerate type. Probably fashion decreed that convinced adherents of the doctrine should be made to ape the countenance and figure, as well as the religion, of their royal teachers, whom the true courtier would vow to be the mirrors of all beauty as well as truth.

Akhenaton: "The First Doctrinaire"

It is on the walls of these tombs, too (for they were spared as inviolable houses of the dead when the temples of the Aten were destroyed), that we read the beautiful hymns to the sun-disk that were composed by the poet-king himself. Their phraseology is strangely reminiscent of that of Psalm 104. . . . Alas for the poet-king! His kingdom had already fallen into anarchy, and the foreign empire which his predecessors had built up had been thrown to the winds in his pursuit of his beautiful ideal. . . . Akhenaten died young and probably insane after a reign of some eighteen years. . . . The whole story is an example of the confusion and disorgani-zation which, *pace* Plato, always ensue when a philosopher rules. Not long after the heretic's early death, the old religion was fully restored, the cult of the disk was blotted out, and the Egyptians returned joyfully to the worship of their myriad deities. Akhenaten's ideals were too high for them. The debris of the foreign empire was, as usual in such cases, put together again, and customary, conventional law and order restored by the stupid, conservative reactionaries who succeeded him. Henceforward, Egyptian civilization ran an uninspired and undeveloping course till the days of the Saites and the Ptolemies.

JOHN A. WILSON

AKHENATON: MONOTHEIST OR HENOTHEIST?

A distinguished American scholar, John A. Wilson is a former Director of the Oriental Institute of the University of Chicago. His illuminating study, *The Burden of Egypt* (1951) (also available as *The Culture of Ancient Egypt*), is both stimulating and sound. A student of Breasted, Wilson recalls the great Egyptologist fondly: "He was persuasive: after forty years, I have some sense of apology if I cannot accept his high evaluation of the revolutionary Pharaoh Akhenaton or if I do not believe that conscience dawned for man pre-eminently in ancient Egypt. He offered his best for us to share."[1] However, Wilson's calm analysis of the Aton cult is more useful than Breasted's rhapsodic hero worship.

With certain exceptions . . . the Amarna texts omit mention of any gods except the Aton. . . . A violent change was the suppression of the former mortuary religion, with all its elaborate formulation centering on the god Osiris. Mortuary prayers and formulas were not now addressed to Osiris or Anubis, but directly to the pharaoh Akhenaton or through him to the Aton. . . . The most important observation about Amarna religion is that there were two gods central to the faith, and not one. Akhenaton and his family worshipped the Aton, and everybody else worshipped Akhenaton *as a god*. In addition to his formal names and titles, the pharaoh was referred to as "the good god," and he asserted that he was the physical son of the Aton. The abundant scenes in the Amarna tombs show him serving the living sun-disk, while all of his courtiers bow in adoration to him. Their prayers were not addressed to the Aton but directly to Akhenaton. The courtier Eye, who was later to become pharaoh, asked Akhenaton for mortuary benefits: "Mayest thou grant to me a good old age as thy favorite; mayest thou grant to me a goodly burial by the command of thy [spirit] in my house. . . . May I hear thy sweet voice in the sanctuary when thou performest that which pleases thy

[1] John A. Wilson, *Signs and Wonders Upon Pharaoh: A History of American Egyptology*, (Chicago: University of Chicago Press, 1964), p. 142.

Reprinted from *The Burden of Egypt* by John A. Wilson, pp. 221–229, by permission of the University of Chicago Press. Copyright © 1951 by the University of Chicago Press.

father, the living Aton." Another noble did pray to the Aton, but prayed only on behalf of Akhenaton, with his petition for himself addressed to the pharaoh: "Mayest thou make thy beloved son Akhenaton to live with thee forever, to do what thy heart wishes, and to behold what thou dost every day, for he rejoices in the sight of thy beauty. . . . Let him remain here, until the swan turns black, until the raven turns white, until the mountains stand up to walk, and until the sea runs up the river. And may I continue in service of the good god Akhenaton until he assigns to me the burial that he gives." This is a stated acknowledgement of the centrality of the pharaoh in the worship of the Aton and of the dependence of the noble upon his god-king. . . . The Aton faith had no penetration below the level of the royal family as an effective religious expression; it was stated to be the exclusive faith of the god-king and his divine family, and the god-king welcomed and encouraged his subjects' worship of his divine being as the source of all the benefits which they might desire.

The self-centered nature of Akhenaton's faith, the fact that only the royal family had a trained and reasoned loyalty to the Aton, and the fact that all of pharaoh's adherents were forced to give their entire devotion to him as a god-king explain why the new religion collapsed after Akhenaton's death. Political and economic factors were also important, but . . . we cannot believe that [the courtiers] cherished within their bosoms the teaching about a benevolent and sustaining sole god, the Aton, when all of their religious exercise was exhausted in worship of Akhenaton. When that pharaoh died and the movement collapsed, they must have scrambled penitently back into the traditional faith, which they could understand and in which they were allowed wider devotion.

Two important questions face us. Was this monotheism? If so, was it the world's first ancestral monotheism, and did it come down to us through the Hebrews? Our own answer to each question is in the negative, even though such an answer may rest upon definitions of the terms, and such definitions must necessarily be those of modern distinctions.

Our modern Jewish, Christian, and Moslem faiths express the doctrine that there is one—and only one—God and that all ethical and religious values derive from that God. In . . . the Amarna religion,

we see that there were at least two gods, that the Aton was concerned strictly with creating and maintaining life, and that ethics and religion derived from the pharaoh Akhenaton. . . . The Amarna texts call the Aton the "sole god, like whom there is no other." This, however, was nothing new in Egyptian religious address. The form of expression was a fervid exaggeration or concentration, which went back to the earliest religious literature more than a thousand years before Akhenaton's time. In the period before the Amarna revolution, Amon, Re, Atum, Har-akhti, and Min were severally called "the sole god." Sometimes this term recalled the creation, when the one existent god was going to bring other gods into being. Sometimes it was a flattering exaggeration meaning the only important god, *like whom* there was no other. Often it was a focusing of the worshipper's attention upon one god, to the exclusion of others—what is called henotheism or monolatry. In no sense does it imply the absolute unity carried by the Moslem: "There is no god but God." In ancient times a man's name was a vital part of his being. . . . The same psychology applies to Akhenaton's attack upon Amon and topically upon other gods. If the philosophy of the new religion was that only the Aton was a god and that, therefore, Amon did not and could not exist, why was there so virulent an attack upon Amon, and why was his name systematically hacked out of the records? In those ancient terms he had still some kind of existence as long as his name was effectively a part of a single record. . . .

Atonism was at one and the same time native to Egyptian religion and unique within that religion. It was native because the Egyptian state was built upon the dogma that pharaoh was a god and stood between the people and the other gods; thus the double relationship at Amarna retained the past essentials. It was unique because the gods other than pharaoh were made one god, by a process of exclusion rather than syncretism. . . . Much more important was the elimination of Osiris from the mortuary faith, with the ascription of all mortuary benefits to the pharaoh. One could say that it was the closest approach to monotheism possible within the thought of the day. That would still fall short of making it a belief in and worship of only one god.

The question as to whether Atonism was ancestral to Hebrew monotheism and thus to modern expressions of religion is also difficult. However, it may be stated flatly that the mechanism of transmission from the faith of Akhenaton to the monotheism of Moses is not apparent. This was the personal religion of a pharaoh who later became a heretic within one generation. It was not accessible to Egyptians at large. Their subsequent reaction in a fervent return to the older forms, particularly the Osirian faith and the cherishing care of little personal gods, shows how little penetration Atonism had below the royal family. Even assuming that there were Israelite slave troops in Egypt in Amarna times, there was no way by which they could learn the teaching of Atonism, that there was a single, universal god, who made and continued life, toward whom the worshipper felt a warm sense of gratitude. Atonism taught that the pharaoh of Egypt was essential as the only intermediary between god and people. There is another discontinuity between Atonism and Hebrew monotheism as the latter developed, and that is the marked lack of ethical content in the hymns directed to the Aton. Akhenaton's faith was intellectual rather than ethical; its strong emotional content derived from the fervor of the discoverer and convert, who rejected past forms and preached new forms. The conviction of right and wrong was not ethical, but was a passionate reiteration that the new was right and the old was wrong. . . . The universalism of the Aton could have carried the implication that all men are equal under the god and should be so treated, but such a logical conclusion is strikingly absent from the texts. . . .

Much of the importance of the Hebrews to world history lies in the fact that they avoided some of the weakening and distracting phases of civilization. A concept which was imperfectly articulated and understood at pharaoh's court at Amarna would have been quite foreign to Asiatic tribes wandering in the desert. When the Children of Israel penetrated Canaan and settled down to work out a new way of life, their progressive religious steps were achieved through their own national religious experience as their own God-given discoveries, without derivation from any foreign source. Such precious and inner expressions of religion can never be borrowed, but must be experienced. When they have been experienced, the *forms* in which they are uttered may be borrowed from others, but never the innermost spirit.

This brings us to a main argument for the contact between Atonism and Hebrew religion: the extraordinary parallelism in thought and structure between Akhenaton's hymn to the Aton and the 104th Psalm. . . . It has been claimed that such correspondences must show derivative connection and that the Hebrew psalmists must have known the Egyptian sun-hymn. Since the obliteration of Atonism was complete some six or seven centuries before the psalm was written, it is argued that the Aton hymn must have passed into Asia when Akhenaton was still in power and escaped destruction by translation into some Semitic dialect. So ingenious a mechanism of transmission is not necessary. We have already seen that the several ideas and modes of expression visible in Atonism were present in Egypt before Atonism and independent of Atonism. Since these were current forms in Egypt, not invented by the Amarna priests or scribes, it is not surprising to find them still in use after the fall of Atonism and without relation to the fact that the specific cult had been proclaimed a heresy. . . . [Wilson cites universalistic hymns to Amon from the Nineteenth and Twentieth Dynasties.] This is an adequate explanation of the similarity between the Aton hymn and the 104th Psalm. Hymns of this kind were current long after the fall of Akhenaton, so that when Hebrew religion had reached a point where it needed a certain mode of expression it could find in another literature phrases and thoughts which would meet the need.

2

DEMOCRACY IN ATHENS

It comes as a surprise to many moderns to learn that democracy has not always been looked upon with favor by Americans. Most of the founding fathers agreed with James Madison that "democracies have ever been spectacles of turbulence and contention, have ever been found incompatible with personal security or the rights of property, and have in general been as short in their lives as they have been violent in their deaths." Even today, some disenchanted people endorse H. L. Mencken's definition of democracy as "the art and science of running the circus from the monkey-cage," though it is doubtful that the wolf's lair or the snake pit would be any improvement. Madison and his contemporaries had never seen a democracy in action and had to rely on the classic historians of Greece who portrayed ancient democracy in dark colors. Later, the excesses of the French Revolution seemed to confirm the standing indictment of democracy as irresponsible and bloody, but the same reasoning ought also to have discredited Christianity since millions have been butchered in the name of the Prince of Peace. The crimes of states have less to do with forms of government than with the personalities of rulers and the imagined needs of the moment. In all fairness, democrats have spilled less blood than barons, bishops, and kings, and popular governments have generally reduced the misery which burdens most men throughout history.

Though there have been "democratic" elements in many societies of the past, true democracy existed only in a few Greek cities which utilized the full participation of all citizens in government. Such total democracy is impractical in large nations which must settle for representative government, but the Greek city-states were small and every citizen was important in politics. The apathy of many modern citizens was foreign to the Greeks who were fervent, even fanatical, in the exercise of their political rights. At times, political passions boiled over into outright factional warfare, and the cities were torn by civil strife. Yet Athens remained relatively free from the horrors of class war. At the city of Miletus, the democrats once trampled the children of oligarchs with oxen, and the oligarchs in turn coated the children of democrats with pitch and turned them into human torches. At no time did the Athenians descend to such atrocities, though Attic democracy was often endangered by oligarchic conspiracies and conservative secret societies whose members took solemn oaths to subvert democracy. We are singularly well informed on the political history of Athens, because of the histories, pamphlets, and philosophic studies which have survived from the era of democracy in Athens. However, the historians and political scientists who are the main sources for the history of Athens were usually unfriendly toward the theory and practice of democracy.

Popular government at Athens was a response to the failures of the Solonian constitution. In 594 B.C. Solon had established a political order in which decision making was in the hands of property owners and only the very wealthy were eligible to be magistrates. Under Solon's system, the masses elected their rulers and could punish them later for abuses of authority; the common people also had control of the courts, for they filled the large juries which decided all cases. By the middle of the sixth century, an able tyrant seized power and ruled Athens without disturbing the forms of Solon's constitution. The tyrant's henchmen filled important offices and executed his wishes. However, circumstances forced the next tyrant to raise taxes and impose a reign of terror against imagined enemies. His real foes soon overthrew him with military aid from Sparta. Though the Spartans preferred an oligarchic regime in Athens, the oligarchs overplayed their hand and were driven from the city about 508 B.C. The victor in the civil strife was a wealthy aristocrat, Cleisthenes, who established the democratic system in Athens with an emphasis on the equality and full participation of all citizens in government. Attic democracy gained great prestige by repulsing two Persian invasions—the naval victory in 480 B.C. was an additional boon to the democrats, for the common people manned the ships which defeated the fleets of Xerxes at Salamis. In the aftermath of the Persian wars, Athens became an imperial power in the Aegean area, extorting tribute from numerous cities which were nominally its allies.

Under the leadership of Pericles, Attic democracy was prosperous and powerful, and the citizens of Athens enjoyed a "Golden Age" of art and drama. In 431 B.C. Athens and Sparta blundered into a major conflict, the Peloponnesian War, which ended in 404 with the defeat of Athens and the loss of its empire. During the stresses of the long war, many Attic conservatives were pro-Spartan and hoped to bring peace by overthrowing the democracy. In 411 B.C. a group of extremists seized control of Athens, but more moderate conservatives gained the upper hand and democracy was restored within a year. In postwar Athens, the Spartans imposed a reactionary oligarchy on the defeated city. The oligarchic regime was called the Thirty and was led by a vicious extremist, Critias, whose purges led to a democratic counterrevolution. By 403 B.C. even the Spartans were disgusted with the Thirty and allowed the democrats to regain the city after a brief civil war. Disdaining reprisals, the restored democracy was remarkably restrained, and the conservative Plato praised it for not massacring its opponents. During the fourth century, Athens did not recover its former power, but democracy flourished despite the complaints of the rich who had to contribute more taxes in the absence of imperial tribute. The great orator Demosthenes warned that Athens and democracy were endangered by the aggressive plans of Philip of Macedon. In 338 B.C. Philip defeated the Athenians at the battle of Chaeronea and established a hegemony over the city-states of Greece. After Alexander, Macedonian warlords imposed oligarchy on Athens in 322 and 317 B.C., but the democrats finally regained control of the city. However, in the Hellenistic age the political life of Athens was irrelevant, for the city's policies were dictated by the kings of the powerful new nations which had been carved from Alexander's empire.

Most discussions of Attic democracy deal with the fifth century B.C., and a brief survey of the political system at the time of Pericles might be useful. All authority rested with the Assembly, which was a legislative body open to all adult male citizens. Anyone might address the Assembly, and its laws and decrees were literally the will of the people. However, the agenda for the Assembly was prepared by the Council of Five Hundred, whose members were chosen by lot. Through astute gerrymandering, the Council was a representative body reflecting the varied economic and geographic interests in the population of Attica. The urban masses of Athens packed the Assembly, but the Council protected rural voters and was largely controlled by machine politicians. The magistrates of Athens performed routine administrative duties and were chosen by lot, but decisions at the executive level were made by a board of ten elected generals, who were both military commanders and political bosses. For thirty years, Pericles dominated Athens as chairman of the board of generals. Because the empire provided prosperity, Periclean democracy had a middle-class tone, and wealthy men directed the destiny of the city. The poor manned the fleet, voted in the Assembly, could serve on the Council, and made up the juries whose activities had expanded since lawsuits involving residents of subject cities were heard at Athens. Imperial tribute paid the meager salaries of magistrates, military men, councilmen, and jurors; in the early fourth century, assemblymen also received a small pay for attendance. A distinctive characteristic of Attic life was the voluntary assumption by the rich of the cost of producing plays and supplying warships for the city. In the fifth century, wealthy men competed for the honor and prestige of such obligations, which became onerous in the fourth century.

Three aspects of Athenian democracy—the lot, ostracism, and demagogues—have often excited critics. In theory, the use of the lot in selecting magistrates and councilmen reflects a naïve faith in the equality of men, but in practice all Athenian officials, whether selected or elected, were first screened by the Council of Five Hundred as to their suitability. On a number of occasions, the voters of Athens ostracized prominent politicians, who were ordered to leave Attica but did not suffer the loss of their property. The pretext for ostracism was that the politician in question was a potential tyrant or a threat to the public weal. In theory, the device seems an absurd attack on talent, a weapon of the jealous masses against a man of ability. But, in practice the vote was instigated and rigged by rival leaders who would be eclipsed by the triumph of one man or who simply wished to break his political influence for a time. The Assembly was often swayed by glib orators who blocked the aims of the Council and the generals by eloquent speeches on the floor of the Assembly. Through oratory a politician could challenge the political machine by appealing to the sovereign people. Critics called the orators "demagogues" and claimed that they confused the electorate with rhetoric and emotion. Yet, politicians in any era employ emotional bombast to obscure issues and convince voters. Demagoguery is effective oratory, and an orator should be censured only if the policy he advocates is wrong or based on lies.

As an imperial power, Athens dealt high-handedly with its subjects and exploited them as do all empires. But the Attic fleet suppressed piracy in the Aegean and the subject cities prospered while they grumbled. In war the Assembly often made wrong decisions and at times acted cruelly, but what nation at war has not stained its hands with innocent blood? Compared to Sparta, the Athenian yoke was light and its crimes were few. A more cogent criticism of Attic democracy would take note of the lack of inherent human rights, for all rights were derived from society and could be abrogated by the state. No Athenian derived rights from his existence as a man. When faced with unjust laws, even Socrates could only say, "Change the laws or obey them." His own martyrdom was a private demonstration of philosophic faith and not an act of civil disobedience. His enemies and friends alike expected the aged philosopher to go into exile, but he wished to prove that a good man will die for the truth. Like Jesus, Socrates sought his own death, and his tragic fate was a glaring exception to the freedom of speech which was one of the glories of Athenian democracy. In the annals of muzzling men and censoring ideas, Athens stands indicted on a few occasions, but the record of Attic democracy is spotless compared to that of imperial Rome, medieval and modern Europe, and most nations today. Even if all were true that the critics of Athens have claimed, we can only concede with Winston Churchill that "democracy is the worst form of government except all those other forms that have been tried from time to time." Too often, moderns forget this simple truth.

"THE OLD OLIGARCH"

A SARCASTIC VIEW OF DEMOCRATIC ATHENS

Though this essay on the practice of democracy at Athens was preserved among the writings of the historian Xenophon, it is obviously the work of a conservative Athenian of the preceding generation who wrote before the Peloponnesian War. The anonymous author has aptly been nicknamed "the Old Oligarch," for he was no friend of democracy. Greek political polemics were generally abusive, but the Old Oligarch was a man of wit who employed sarcasm effectively. Instead of theorizing about the virtues of oligarchy, the author describes the fallible workings of democracy with graphic realism. Despite his hostile tone, he offers a rare glimpse of Athens in the fifth century B.C. In the following passages, the term "the People" stands interchangeably for the popular faction, the Athenian masses, and the Assembly which they controlled through their votes.

Now, as for the constitution of the Athenians and the type or manner of constitution which they have chosen, I praise it not, in so far as the very choice involves the welfare of the baser folk as opposed to that of the better class. I repeat, I withhold my praise so far; but, given the fact that this is the type agreed

From "The Old Oligarch," *The Constitution of the Athenians,* tr. Henry G. Dakyns, in *The Greek Historians,* edited by Francis R. B. Godolphin, Vol. II, pp. 633–37, 640–41. Copyright 1942 by Random House, Inc. Reprinted by permission.

upon, I propose to show that they set about its preservation in the right way; and that those other transactions in connection with it, which are looked upon as blunders by the rest of the Hellenic world, are the reverse.

In the first place, I maintain, it is only just that the poorer classes and the common people of Athens should be better off than the men of birth and wealth, seeing that it is the people who man the fleet and have brought the city her power. . . . This being the case, it seems only just that offices of state should be thrown open to every one both in the ballot and the show of hands, and that the right of speech should belong to any one who likes, without restriction. For, observe, there are many of these offices which, according as they are in good or in bad hands, are a source of safety or of danger to the People, and in these the People prudently abstains from sharing; as, for instance, it does not think it incumbent on itself to share in the functions of the general or of the commander of cavalry. The commons recognizes the fact that in forgoing the personal exercise of these offices and leaving them to the control of the more powerful citizens, it secures the balance of advantage to itself. It is only those departments of government which bring pay and assist the private estate that the People cares to keep in its own hands.

In the next place . . . . the fact that everywhere greater consideration is shown to the base, to poor people and to common folk, than to persons of good quality—so far from being a matter of surprise, this, as can be shown, is the keystone of the preservation of the democracy. It is these poor people, this common folk, this worse element, whose prosperity, combined with the growth of their numbers, enhances the democracy. . . . In fact, all the world over, the cream of society is in opposition to the democracy. Naturally, since the smallest amount of intemperance and injustice, together with the highest scrupulousness in the pursuit of excellence, is to be found in the ranks of the better class, while within the ranks of the People will be found the greatest amount of ignorance, disorderliness, rascality—poverty acting as a stronger incentive to base conduct, not to speak of lack of education and ignorance, traceable to the lack of means which afflicts the average of mankind.

The objection may be raised that it was a mistake to allow the universal right of speech and a seat in council. These should have been reserved for the cleverest, the flower of the community. But here, again, it will be found that they are acting with wise deliberation in granting to even the baser sort the right of speech, for supposing only the better people might speak or sit in council, blessings would fall to the lot of those like themselves, but to the commons the reverse of blessings. Whereas now, any one who likes, any base fellow, may get up and discover something to the advantage of himself and his equals. It may be retorted, "And what sort of advantage either for himself or for the People can such a fellow be expected to hit upon?" The answer to which is, that in their judgment the ignorance and the baseness of this fellow, together with his goodwill, are worth a great deal more to them than your superior person's virtue and wisdom, coupled with animosity. What it comes to, therefore, is that a state founded upon such institutions will not be the best state; but, given a democracy, these are the right means to secure its preservation. The People, it must be borne in mind, does not demand that the city should be well governed and itself a slave. It desires to be free and to be master. As to bad legislation, it does not concern itself about that. In fact, what you believe to be bad legislation is the very source of the People's strength and freedom. But if you seek for good legislation, in the first place you will see the cleverest members of the community laying down the laws for the rest. And in the next place, the better class will curb and chastise the lower orders; the better class will deliberate in behalf of the state and not suffer crack-brained fellows to sit in council or to speak or vote in the assemblies. No doubt; but under the weight of such blessings, the People will in a very short time be reduced to slavery.

Another point is the extraordinary amount of license granted to slaves and resident aliens at Athens, where a blow is illegal and a slave will not step aside to let you pass him in the street. . . . Supposing it were legal for a slave to be beaten by a free citizen or for a resident alien or freedman to be beaten by a citizen, it would frequently happen that an Athenian might be mistaken for a slave or an alien and receive a beating; since the Athenian People is not better clothed than the slave or alien, nor in personal appearance is there any superiority. . . . Slaves in Athens are allowed to indulge in luxury and . . . we must perforce be slaves to our slaves, in order that we may get in our slave-rents. . . . Where you have wealthy slaves it ceases to be advantageous that my slave should stand in awe of you. In [Sparta] my slave stands in awe of you. But if your slave is in awe of me, there will be a risk of his giving away his own moneys to avoid running a risk in his own person. It is for this reason then that we have established an equality between our slaves and free men, and again between our resident aliens and full citizens, because the city stands in need of her resident aliens to meet the requirements of such a multiplicity of arts and for the purposes of her navy. . . .

The common people put a stop to citizens devoting their time to athletics and to the cultivation of music, disbelieving in the beauty of such training, and recognizing the fact that these are things the cultivation of which is beyond its power. On the same principle, in the case of the [chorus producer], the management of athletics, and the command of ships, the fact is recognized that it is the rich man who trains the chorus and the People for whom the chorus is trained; it is the rich man who is naval commander or superintendent of athletics, and the People that profits by their labors. In fact, what the People looks upon as its right is to pocket the money. To sing and run and dance and man the vessels is well enough, but only in order that the People may be the gainer, while the rich are made poorer. And so in the courts of justice, justice is not more an object of concern to the jurymen than what touches personal advantage. . . .

Again, it is looked upon as a mistaken policy on the part of the Athenian democracy to compel her allies to voyage to Athens in order to have their cases tried. On the other hand, it is easy to reckon up what a number of advantages the Athenian People derives from the practice impugned. In the first place, there is the steady receipt of salaries throughout the year derived from the court fees. Next, it enables them to manage the affairs of the allied states while seated at home without the expense of naval expeditions. Thirdly, they thus preserve the partisans of the democracy, and ruin her opponents in the law courts. Whereas, supposing the several allied states tried their cases at home, being inspired by hostility to Athens, they would destroy those of their own citizens whose friendship to the Athenian People was most marked. But besides all this, the democracy derives the following advantages from hearing the cases of her allies in Athens. In the first place, the one per cent [tax] levied in Piraeus is increased to the profit of the state; again, the owner of a lodging-house does better, and so, too, the owner of a pair of beasts or of slaves to be let out on hire; again, heralds and criers are a class of people who fare better owing to the sojourn of foreigners at Athens. . . . Every single individual among the allies is forced to pay flattery to the People of Athens because he knows that he must betake himself to Athens and win or lose his case at the bar, not of any stray set of judges, but of the sovereign People itself, such being the law and custom at Athens. He is compelled to behave as a suppliant in the courts of justice and, when some juryman comes into court, to grasp his hand. . . .

In the case of engagements entered into by a democracy, it is open to the People to throw the blame on the single individual who spoke in favor of some measure, or put it to the vote, and to maintain to the rest of the world, "I was not present, nor do I approve of the terms of the agreement." Inquiries are made in a full meeting of the People, and should any of these things be disapproved of, they can at once discover countless excuses to avoid doing whatever they do not wish. And if any mischief should spring out of any resolutions which the People has passed in council, the People can readily shift the blame from its own shoulders: "A handful of oligarchs acting against the interests of the People have ruined us." But if any good result ensue, they, the People, at once take the credit of that to themselves.

In the same spirit, it is not allowed to caricature on the comic stage or otherwise libel the People, because they do not care to hear themselves ill spoken of. But if any one has a desire to satirize his neighbor he has full leave to do so. And this because they are well aware that, as a general rule, the person caricatured does not belong to the People. . . . He is more likely to be some wealthy or well-born person or man of means and influence. In fact, but few poor people and of the popular stamp incur the comic lash, or if they do they have brought it on themselves by excessive love of meddling or some covetous self-seeking at the expense of the People, so that no particular annoyance is felt at seeing such folk satirized.

What, then, I venture to assert is, that the People of Athens has no difficulty in recognizing which of its citizens are of the better sort and which the opposite. And so recognizing those who are serviceable and advantageous to itself, even though they be base, the People loves them; but the good folk they are disposed . . . to hate. This virtue of theirs, the People holds, is not engrained in their nature for any good to itself, but rather for its injury. . . . For my part, I pardon the People its own democracy, as, indeed it is pardonable in any one to do good to himself. But the man who, not being himself one of the People, prefers to live in a state democratically governed rather than in an oligarchical state may be said to smooth his own path towards iniquity. He knows that a bad man has a better chance of slipping through the fingers of justice in a democratic . . . state. . . .

It not seldom happens, they tell us, that a man is unable to transact a piece of business with the [Council of Five Hundred or the Assembly], even if he sits waiting a whole year. Now this does happen at Athens, and for no other reason save that, owing to the immense mass of affairs they are unable to work off all the business on hand and dismiss the applicants. And how in the world should they be able, considering in the first place that they, the Athenians, have more festivals to celebrate than any other

state . . . of Hellas? . . . In the next place, only consider the number of cases they have to decide, what with private suits and public causes and scrutinies of accounts, more than the whole of the rest of mankind put together; while the [Council] has multifarious points to advise upon concerning peace and war, concerning ways and means, concerning the framing and passing of laws, and concerning the matters affecting the state perpetually occurring, and endless questions touching the allies; besides the receipt of the tribute, the superintendence of dockyards and temples. Can, I ask again, any one find it at all surprising that, with all these affairs on their hands, they are unequal to doing business with all the world? But some people tell us that if the applicant will only address himself to the [Council or the Assembly] with a bribe in his hand, he will do a good stroke of business. And for my part I am free to confess . . . that a good many things may be done at Athens by dint of money. . . . However, . . . as to transacting with every one of these applicants all he wants, the state could not do it, not even if all the gold and silver in the world were the inducement offered.

THUCYDIDES

FACTIONAL WARFARE ON CORCYRA

During the Peloponnesian War between Athens and Sparta, both sides tried to justify their war aims with ideological slogans—the Spartans posed as the liberators of Hellas while the Athenians claimed to be fighting for democracy. In 427 B.C. the democrats on the island of Corcyra took advantage of Athenian protection to massacre their oligarchic "pro-Spartan" opponents. The savage episode gave the great historian Thucydides an opportunity to digress on the grim nature of factional strife everywhere in Hellas. Born of a wealthy conservative Athenian family, Thucydides was critical of democratic errors but he admired Pericles and approved of a limited democracy in which the franchise would be restricted to property holders. When he composed this passage, postwar Athens was in the hands of a group of reactionary oligarchs, the Thirty, who ruthlessly purged the supporters of democracy. Thucydides intended his digression on Corcyra as a rebuke to all such bloodletting by either political faction.

When the Corcyraeans perceived that the Athenian fleet was approaching, while that of the enemy had disappeared, they . . . killed any of their enemies whom they caught in the city. . . . They also went to the temple of Hera and persuading about fifty of the suppliants to stand their trial, condemned them all to death. The majority would not come out, and, when they saw what was going on, destroyed one another in the enclosure of the temple where they were, except a few who hung themselves on trees or put an end to their own lives in any other way which they could. And during the seven days [while the Athenian squadron remained in the harbor], the Corcyraeans continued slaughtering those of their fellow-citizens whom they deemed their enemies; they professed to punish them for their designs against the democracy, but in fact some were killed from motives of personal enmity, and some because money was owing to them, by the hands of their debtors. Every form of death was to be seen, and everything, and more than everything that commonly happens in revolutions, happened then. The father slew the son, and the suppliants were torn from the temples and slain near them; some of them were even walled up in the temple of Dionysus and there perished. To such extremes of cruelty did revolution go, and this seemed to be the worst of revolutions because it was the first.

For not long afterwards the whole Hellenic world was in commotion; in every city the chiefs of the democracy and of the oligarchy were struggling, the one to bring in the Athenians, the other the [Spartans]. . . . In time of peace, men would have had no excuse for introducing either, and no desire to do so, but when they were at war and both sides could easily obtain allies to the hurt of their enemies and the advantage of themselves, the dissatisfied party were only too ready to invoke foreign aid. And revolution brought upon the cities of Hellas many terrible calamities, such as have been and always will be while human nature remains the same, but which are more or less aggravated and differ in character with every new combination of circumstances. In peace and prosperity, both states and individuals are actuated by higher motives, because they do not fall under the dominion of imperious necessities; but war which takes away the comfortable provision of daily life is a hard master and tends to assimilate men's characters to their conditions.

When troubles had once begun in the cities, those who followed carried the revolutionary spirit further and further, and determined to outdo the report of all who had preceded them by the ingenuity of their enterprises and the atrocity of their revenges. The meaning of words had no longer the same relation to things, but was changed by them as they thought proper. Reckless daring was held to be loyal courage; prudent delay was the excuse of a coward; moderation was the disguise of unmanly weakness; to know everything was to do nothing. Frantic energy was the true quality of a man. A conspirator who wanted to be safe was a recreant in disguise. The lover of violence was always trusted, and his opponent suspected. He who succeeded in a plot was deemed knowing, but a still greater master in craft was he who detected one. On the other hand, he who plotted from the first to have nothing to do with plots was a breaker up of parties and a poltroon who was afraid of the enemy. In a word, he who could outstrip another in a bad action was applauded, and so was he who encouraged to evil one who had no idea of it. The tie of party was stronger than the tie of blood, because a partisan was more ready to dare without asking why. (For party associations are not based upon any established law, nor do they seek the public good; they are formed in defiance of the laws and from self-interest.) The seal of good faith was not divine law but fellowship in crime. If any enemy when he was in the ascendant offered fair words, the opposite party received them not in a generous spirit but by a jealous watchfulness of his actions. Revenge was dearer than self-preservation. Any agreements sworn to by either party, when they could do nothing else, were binding as long as both were powerless. But he who on a favorable opportunity first took courage and struck at his enemy when he saw him off his guard, had greater pleasure in a perfidious than he would have had in an open act of revenge; he congratulated himself that he had taken the safer course, and also that he had overreached his enemy and gained the prize of superior ability. In general the dishonest more easily gain credit for cleverness than the simple for goodness; men take a pride in the one but are ashamed of the other.

The cause of all these evils was the love of power, originating in avarice and ambition, and the party-spirit which is engendered by them when men are fairly embarked in a contest. For the leaders on either side used specious names, the one party professing to uphold the constitutional equality of the many, the other the wisdom of an aristocracy, while they made the public interests, to which in name they were devoted, in reality their prize. Striving in every way to overcome each other, they committed

From Thucydides, III, 81–84, translated by Benjamin Jowett, in *The Greek Historians*, edited by Francis R. B. Godolphin, Vol. I, pp. 719–22. Copyright 1942 by Random House, Inc. Reprinted by permission.

the most monstrous crimes; yet even these were surpassed by the magnitude of their revenges which they pursued to the very utmost, neither party observing any definite limits either of justice or public expediency, but both alike making the caprice of the moment their law. Either by the help of an unrighteous sentence or grasping power with the strong hand, they were eager to satiate the impatience of party-spirit. Neither faction cared for religion, but any fair pretence which succeeded in effecting some odious purpose was greatly lauded. And the citizens who were of neither party fell a prey to both; either they were disliked because they held aloof, or men were jealous of their surviving.

Thus revolution gave birth to every form of wickedness in Hellas. The simplicity which is so large an element in a noble nature was laughed to scorn and disappeared. An attitude of perfidious antagonism everywhere prevailed, for there was no word binding enough, nor oath terrible enough to reconcile enemies. Each man was strong only in the conviction that nothing was secure; he must look to his own safety and could not afford to trust others. Inferior intellects generally succeeded best. For, aware of their own deficiencies and fearing the capacity of their opponents, for whom they were no match in powers of speech and whose subtle wits were likely to anticipate them in contriving evil, they struck boldly and at once. But the cleverer sort, presuming in their arrogance that they would be aware in time and disdaining to act when they could think, were taken off their guard and easily destroyed.

Now in Corcyra most of these deeds were perpetrated and for the first time. There was every crime which men might be supposed to perpetrate in revenge who had been governed not wisely but tyrannically, and now had the oppressor at their mercy. There were the dishonest designs of others who were longing to be relieved from their habitual poverty and were naturally animated by a passionate desire for their neighbor's goods; and there were crimes of another class which men commit not from covetousness but from the enmity which equals foster towards one another until they are carried away by their blind rage into the extremes of pitiless cruelty. At such a time the life of the city was all in disorder, and human nature, which is always ready to transgress the laws, having now trampled them under foot, delighted to show that her passions were ungovernable, that she was stronger than justice, and the enemy of everything above her. If malignity had not exercised a fatal power, how could any one have preferred revenge to piety, and gain to innocence? But, when men are retaliating upon others, they are reckless of the future and do not hesitate to annul those common laws of humanity to which every individual trusts for his own hope of deliverance should he ever be overtaken by calamity; they forget that in their own hour of need they will look to them in vain.[1]

[1] This last paragraph (III 84) may have been inserted by an ancient editor of the text. [Editor's note.]

GEORGE GROTE

A NINETEENTH-CENTURY LIBERAL DEFENDS

DEMOCRATIC ATHENS

The classic English history of Greece was composed by George Grote (1794–1871). Appearing in twelve volumes from 1846 to 1856, his *History of Greece* was a masterful work backed by sound scholarship and common sense and full of valuable insights. Though his treatment of some topics naturally is dated, the book has survived the passage of time remarkably well and is still useful for modern students. A successful banker and member of Parliament, Grote had an abiding interest in politics, ancient and modern. More liberal than his fellow members of the Liberal Party, he was a fervent believer in popular government and wrote at a time when "democracy happens to be unpalatable to most modern readers." Though he was also an authority on Greek philosophy, Grote felt that the development of democracy at Athens was an even greater achievement than the familiar Greek triumphs in art, thought, and literature.

The fruit of the fresh-planted democracy as well as the seed for its sustenation and aggrandizement continued progressive during the whole period. . . . But the first unexpected burst of it under the Cleisthenean constitution . . . is described by Herodotus in terms too emphatic to be omitted: . . . "Thus did the Athenians grow in strength. And we may find proof, not merely in this instance but everywhere else, how valuable a thing freedom is: since even the Athenians, while under a despot, were not superior in war to any of their surrounding neighbors, but, so soon as they got rid of their despots, became by far the first of all. These things show that while kept down by one man, they were slack and timid like men working for a master; but when they were liberated, every single man became eager in exertions for his own benefit." The same comparison reappears a short time afterwards where he tells us that "the Athenians when free felt themselves a match for Sparta, but while kept down by any man under a despotism, were feeble and apt for submission."

Stronger expressions cannot be found to depict the rapid improvement wrought in the Athenian people by their new democracy. Of course this did not arise merely from suspension of previous cruelties, or better laws, or better administration. These, indeed, were essential conditions, but the active transforming cause here was the principle and system of which such amendments formed the detail: the grand and new idea of the sovereign People, composed of free and equal citizens — or liberty and equality, to use words which so profoundly moved the French nation half a century ago. It was this comprehensive political idea which acted with electric effect upon the Athenians, creating within them a host of sentiments, motives, sympathies, and capacities, to which they had before been strangers. Democracy in Grecian antiquity possessed the privilege, not only of kindling an earnest and unanimous attachment to the constitution in the bosoms of the citizens, but also of creating an energy of public and private action, such as could never be obtained under an oligarchy, where the utmost that could be hoped for was a passive acquiescence and obedi-ence. Mr. [Edmund] Burke has remarked that the mass of the people are generally very indifferent about theories of government; but such indifference — although improvements in the practical working of all governments tend to foster it — is hardly to be expected among any people who exhibit decided mental activity and spirit on other matters; and the reverse was unquestionably true in the year 500 B.C. among the communities of ancient Greece. Theories of government were there anything but a dead letter: they were connected with emotions of the strongest . . . character. The theory of a permanent ruling One, for example, was universally odious: that of a ruling Few, though acquiesced in, was never positively attractive, unless either where it was associated with the maintenance of peculiar education and habits, as at Sparta, or where it presented itself as the only antithesis to democracy, the latter having by peculiar circumstances become an object of terror. But the theory of democracy was preeminently seductive, creating in the mass of the citizens an intense positive attachment and disposing them to voluntary action and suffering on its behalf, such as no coercion on the part of other governments could extort. Herodotus, in his comparison of the three sorts of government, puts in the front rank of the advantages of democracy, "its most splendid name and promise" — its power of enlisting the hearts of the citizens in support of their constitution and of providing for all a common bond of union and fraternity. This is what even democracy did not always do, but it was what no other government in Greece *could* do: a reason alone sufficient to stamp it as the best government and presenting the greatest chance of beneficent results for a Grecian community. Among the Athenian citizens, certainly, it produced a strength and unanimity of positive political sentiment, such as has rarely been seen in the history of mankind, which excites our surprise and admiration the more when we compare it with the apathy which had preceded. . . . Because democracy happens to be unpalatable to most modern readers, they have been accustomed to look upon the sentiment here described only in its least honorable manifestations — in the caricatures of Aristophanes or in the empty

From George Grote, *History of Greece* (London: John Murray, 1847), Vol. IV, pp. 235–242.

commonplaces of rhetorical declaimers. But it is not in this way that the force, the earnestness, or the binding value of democratical sentiment at Athens is to be measured. We must listen to it as it comes from the lips of Pericles, while he is strenuously enforcing upon the people those active duties for which it both implanted the stimulus and supplied the courage; or from the oligarchical Nicias in the harbor of Syracuse, when he is endeavoring to revive the courage of his despairing troops for one last death-struggle, and when he appeals to their democratical patriotism as to the only flame yet alive and burning even in that moment of agony. From the time of Cleisthenes downward, the creation of this new mighty impulse makes an entire revolution in the Athenian character. And if the change still stood out in so prominent a manner before the eyes of Herodotus, much more must it have been felt by the contemporaries among whom it occurred.

The attachment of an Athenian citizen to his democratical constitution comprised two distinct veins of sentiment: first, his rights, protection, and advantages derived from it—next, his obligations of exertion and sacrifice towards it and with reference to it. Neither of these two veins of sentiment was ever wholly absent; but according as the one or the other was present at different times in varying proportions, the patriotism of the citizen was a very different feeling. That which Herodotus remarks is, the extraordinary efforts of heart and hand which the Athenians suddenly displayed—the efficacy of the active sentiment throughout the bulk of the citizens; and we shall observe even more memorable evidences of the same phenomenon in tracing down the history from Cleisthenes to the end of the Peloponnesian War: we shall trace a series of events and motives eminently calculated to stimulate that self-imposed labor and discipline which the early democracy had first called forth. But when we advance farther down from the restoration of the democracy after the Thirty Tyrants to the time of Demosthenes—I venture upon this brief anticipation in the conviction that one period of Grecian history can only be thoroughly understood by contrasting it with another—we shall find a sensible change in Athenian patriotism. The active sentiment of obligation is comparatively inoperative—the citizen, it is true, has a keen sense of the value of the democracy as protecting him and ensuring to him valuable rights, and he is moreover willing to perform his ordinary sphere of legal duties towards it; but he looks upon it as a thing established and capable of maintaining itself in a due measure of foreign ascendency without any such personal efforts as those which his forefathers cheerfully imposed upon themselves. The orations of Demosthenes contain melancholy proofs of such altered tone of patriotism—of that languor, paralysis, and waiting for others to act, which preceded the catastrophe of Chaeronea, notwithstanding an unabated attachment to the democracy as a source of protection and good government. That same preternatural activity which the allies of Sparta at the beginning of the Peloponnesian War both denounced and admired in the Athenians, is noted by the orator as now belonging to their enemy Philip.

Such variations in the scale of national energy pervade history, modern as well as ancient, but in regard to Grecian history especially, they can never be overlooked. For a certain measure, not only of positive political attachment, but also of active self-devotion, military readiness, and personal effort, was the indispensable condition of maintaining Hellenic autonomy either in Athens or elsewhere, and became so more than ever when the Macedonians were once organized under an enterprising and semi-Hellenized prince. The democracy was the first creative cause of that astonishing personal and many-sided energy which marked the Athenian character for a century downward from Cleisthenes. That the same ultra-Hellenic activity did not longer continue, is referable to other causes. . . . No system of government, even supposing it to be very much better and more faultless than the Athenian democracy, can ever pretend to accomplish its legitimate end apart from the personal character of the people or to supersede the necessity of individual virtue and vigor. During the half-century immediately preceding the battle of Chaeronea, the Athenians had lost that remarkable energy which distinguished them during the first century of their democracy and had fallen much more nearly to a level with the other Greeks, in common with whom they were obliged to yield to the pressure of a foreign enemy. I here briefly notice their last period of languor in contrast with the first burst of democratical fervor under Cleisthenes . . .—a feeling which will be found . . . to continue for a longer period than could have been reasonably anticipated, but which was too high-strung to become a perpetual and inherent attribute of any community.

LORD ACTON

ATHENS: THE TYRANNY OF THE MAJORITY

John Emerich Dalberg-Acton, Lord Acton (1834–1902), was Regius Professor of Modern History at Cambridge. He was the author of many articles and essays and the driving force behind the famous reference work *The Cambridge Modern History*. His thoughts on history and liberty have had considerable influence on many moderns. Acton was a fervent libertarian and unalterably opposed any form of authoritarianism, secular or ecclesiastical. As a Catholic in Protestant England, he had felt the weight of official bigotry and was sensitive to the plight of minorities. Acton was equally opposed to papal absolutism and criticized Pius IX and the Vatican Council of 1870. Obsessed with abuses of authority, Acton planned to write a definitive *History of Liberty*, but he never got around to writing it—which is probably just as well since he felt that Thucydides' "judgment in politics is never at fault." The learned baron was blinded by the class prejudices of his time. Though he worshiped liberty with all the fanaticism of a French revolutionary, Acton did not believe in equality and he was not temperamentally inclined toward fraternity.

Liberty, next to religion, has been the motive of good deeds and the common pretext of crime, from the sowing of the seed at Athens, two thousand four hundred and sixty years ago, until the ripened harvest was gathered by men of our race. . . . At all times sincere friends of freedom have been rare, and its triumphs have been due to minorities, that have prevailed by associating themselves with auxiliaries whose objects often differed from their own; and this association, which is always dangerous, has been sometimes disastrous. . . . The most certain test by which we judge whether a country is really free is the amount of security enjoyed by minorities. . . .

Pericles . . . resolutely struck away all the props that still sustained the artificial preponderance of wealth. For the ancient doctrine that power goes with land, he introduced the idea that power ought to be so equitably diffused as to afford equal security to all. That one part of the community should govern the whole, or that one class should make laws for another, he declared to be tyrannical. The abolition of privilege would have served only to transfer the supremacy from the rich to the poor, if Pericles had not redressed the balance by restricting the right of citizenship to Athenians of pure descent. By this measure, the class which formed what we should call the third estate was brought down to 14,000 citizens and became about equal in numbers with the higher ranks. Pericles held that every Athenian who neglected to take his part in the public business inflicted an injury on the commonwealth. That none might be excluded by poverty, he caused the poor to be paid for their attendance out of the funds of the State, for his administration of the federal tribute had brought together a treasure of more than two million sterling. The instrument of his sway was the art of speaking. He governed by persuasion. Everything was decided by argument in open deliberation, and every influence bowed before the ascendancy of mind. The idea that the object of constitutions is not to confirm the predominance of any interest, but to prevent it; to preserve with equal care the independence of labor and the security of property; to make the rich safe against envy and the poor against oppression, marks the highest level attained by the statesmanship of Greece. It hardly survived the great patriot who conceived it; and all history has been occupied with the endeavor to

From John Emerich Edward Dalberg-Acton, First Baron Acton, *The History of Freedom and Other Essays,* eds. John Neville Figgis and Reginald Vere Laurence (London: Macmillan & Co. Ltd., 1907) pp. 1, 9–13, 16–17, 29.

upset the balance of power by giving the advantage to money, land, or numbers. A generation followed that has never been equalled in talent—a generation of men whose works in poetry and eloquence are still the envy of the world, and in history, philosophy, and politics remain unsurpassed. But it produced no successor to Pericles, and no man was able to wield the sceptre that fell from his hand.

It was a momentous step in the progress of nations when the principle that every interest should have the right and the means of asserting itself was adopted by the Athenian Constitution. But for those who were beaten in the vote there was no redress. The law did not check the triumph of majorities or rescue the minority from the dire penalty of having been outnumbered. When the overwhelming influence of Pericles was removed, the conflict between classes raged without restraint, and the slaughter that befell the higher ranks in the Peloponnesian War gave an irresistible preponderance to the lower. The restless and inquiring spirit of the Athenians was prompt to unfold the reason of every institution and the consequences of every principle, and their Constitution ran its course from infancy to decrepitude with unexampled speed. . . .

Their history furnishes the classic example of the peril of Democracy under conditions singularly favorable. For the Athenians were not only brave and patriotic and capable of generous sacrifice, but they were the most religious of the Greeks. They venerated the Constitution which had given them prosperity and equality and freedom, and never questioned the fundamental laws which regulated the enormous power of the Assembly. They tolerated considerable variety of opinion and great license of speech; and their humanity towards their slaves roused the indignation even of the most intelligent partisan of aristocracy. Thus they became the only people of antiquity that grew great by democratic institutions. But the possession of unlimited power, which corrodes the conscience, hardens the heart, and confounds the understanding of monarchs, exercised its demoralizing influence on the illustrious democracy of Athens. It is bad to be oppressed by a minority, but it is worse to be oppressed by a majority. For there is a reserve of latent power in the masses which, if it is called into play, the minority can seldom resist. But from the absolute will of an entire people there is no appeal, no redemption, no refuge but treason. The humblest and most numerous class of the Athenians united the legislative, the

judicial, and, in part, the executive power. The philosophy that was then in the ascendant taught them that there is no law superior to that of the State—the lawgiver is above the law.

It followed that the sovereign people had a right to do whatever was within its power, and was bound by no rule of right or wrong but its own judgment of expediency. On a memorable occasion the assembled Athenians declared it monstrous that they should be prevented from doing whatever they chose. No force that existed could restrain them; and they resolved that no duty should restrain them, and that they would be bound by no laws that were not of their own making. In this way the emancipated people of Athens became a tyrant, and their Government, the pioneer of European freedom, stands condemned with a terrible unanimity by all the wisest of the ancients. They ruined their city by attempting to conduct war by debate in the marketplace. Like the French Republic, they put their unsuccessful commanders to death. They treated their dependencies with such injustice that they lost their maritime empire. They plundered the rich until the rich conspired with the public enemy, and they crowned their guilt by the martyrdom of Socrates.

When the absolute sway of numbers had endured for nearly a quarter of a century, nothing but bare existence was left for the State to lose, and the Athenians, wearied and despondent, confessed the true cause of their ruin. They understood that for liberty, justice, and equal laws, it is as necessary that Democracy should restrain itself as it had been that it should restrain the oligarchy. . . . The repentance of the Athenians came too late to save the Republic. But the lesson of their experience endures for all times, for it teaches that government by the whole people, being the government of the most numerous and most powerful class, is an evil of the same nature as unmixed monarchy and requires, for nearly the same reasons, institutions that shall protect it against itself and shall uphold the permanent reign of law against arbitrary revolutions of opinion. . . .

The ancients understood the regulation of power better than the regulation of liberty. They concentrated so many prerogatives in the State as to leave no footing from which a man could deny its jurisdiction or assign bounds to its activity. If I may employ an expressive anachronism, the vice of the classic state was that it was both Church and

State in one. Morality was undistinguished from religion and politics from morals; and in religion, morality, and politics there was only one legislator and one authority. The State, while it did deplorably little for education, for practical science, for the indigent and helpless, or for the spiritual needs of man, nevertheless claimed the use of all his faculties and the determination of all his duties. Individuals and families, associations and dependencies were so much material that the sovereign power consumed for its own purposes. What the slave was in the hands of his master, the citizen was in the hands of the community. The most sacred obligations vanished before the public advantage. The passengers existed for the sake of the ship. By their disregard for private interests and for the moral welfare and improvement of the people, both Greece and Rome destroyed the vital elements on which the prosperity of nations rests, and perished by the decay of families and the depopulation of the country. They survive not in their institutions but in their ideas, and by their ideas, especially on the art of government, they are—

The dead, but sceptred sovereigns who still rule
Our spirits from their urns.

To them, indeed, may be tracked nearly all the errors that are undermining political society—Communism, Utilitarianism, the confusion between tyranny and political authority, and between lawlessness and freedom. . . . All that Socrates could effect by way of protest against the tyranny of the reformed democracy was to die for his convictions. . . . But when Christ said: "Render unto Caesar the things that are Caesar's, and unto God the things that are God's," those words . . . gave to the civil power, under the protection of conscience, a sacredness it had never enjoyed and bounds it had never acknowledged; and they were the repudiation of absolutism and the inauguration of freedom.

A.H.M. JONES

ATHENIAN DEMOCRACY: CRITICS AND REALITIES

Too often historians have, like Lord Acton, inferred a theory about ancient democracy and then damned the Athenians for adhering to such an absurd idea. However, a historian should be an investigator and not a judge—the nature of the past is complex and not always clear, and nothing is gained by rhetorical attacks on imagined evils. For those who wish to understand democracy at Athens, a safer guide than Acton or Grote is A. H. M. Jones of the University of Cambridge, who is a recognized authority on Greece and Rome. Widely respected for his books and articles, Professor Jones has recently written a monumental study of the later Roman Empire. Though sympathetic to Athenian democracy, he is not a partisan apologist, as Grote sometimes was. With learning and common sense, Jones contrasts the bitter attacks of ancient critics on Athens and the actual operation of democracy in the city.

All the Athenian political philosophers and publicists whose works we possess were in various degrees oligarchic in sympathy. The author of the pamphlet on the "Constitution of the Athenians" preserved among Xenophon's works is bitterly hostile to democracy. Socrates, so far as we can trace his views from the works of Xenophon and Plato, was at least highly critical of democracy. Plato's views on the subject are too well known to need stating. Isocrates in his earlier years wrote pane-

From A. H. M. Jones, *Athenian Democracy* (Oxford, 1957), pp. 41–42, 44–46, 48, 50, 55, 61–62. Reprinted by permission of Basil Blackwell Ltd.

gyrics of Athens, but in his old age, when he wrote his more philosophical works, became increasingly embittered against the political regime of his native city. Aristotle is the most judicial in his attitude and states the pros and cons, but his ideal was a widely based oligarchy. With the historians of Athens, the same bias is evident. Only Herodotus is a democrat, but his views have not carried much weight, partly because of his reputation for naïveté, and partly because his explicit evidence refers to a period before the full democracy had evolved. Thucydides is hostile: in one of the very few passages in which he reveals his personal views, he expresses approval of a regime which disfranchised about two-thirds of the citizens, those who manned the fleet on which the survival of Athens depended. Xenophon was an ardent admirer of the Spartan regime. Aristotle, in the historical part of his monograph on the Constitution of Athens, followed —rather uncritically—a source with a marked oligarchic bias. Only the fourth-century orators were democrats; and their speeches, being concerned with practical political issues—mostly of foreign policy —or with private litigation, have little to say on the basic principles of democracy, which they take for granted.

The surviving literature is certainly not representative of Athenian public opinion. The majority of Athenians were proud of their constitution and deeply attached to it. The few counter-revolutions —in 411, 404, 322, and 317—were carried out by small extremist cliques, in 411 after a carefully planned campaign of deception and terror, in the other three cases with the aid of a foreign conqueror, and all were short-lived, being rapidly overwhelmed by the mass of the citizens. Nor was it only the poor majority, who most obviously benefited from the system, that were its supporters. Most of the great statesmen and generals of Athens came from wealthy families, and a substantial number from the nobility of birth; the leaders of the popular risings which unseated the oligarchic governments of 411 and 403 were men of substance. . . .

Freedom of action and of speech were the proudest slogans of Athens, and not only political but personal freedom; as Pericles says in the Funeral Speech, "we live as free citizens both in our public life and in our attitude to one another in the affairs of daily life; we are not angry with our neighbor if he behaves as he pleases, we do not cast sour looks at him which, if they can do no harm, cause pain."

Freedom of speech was particularly prized. As Demosthenes says, "in Sparta you are not allowed to praise the laws of Athens or of this state or that, far from it, you have to praise what agrees with their constitution," whereas in Athens criticism of the democracy was freely permitted. One only has to read the works of Isocrates, Plato, and Aristotle to see that this is true. The condemnation of Socrates is an apparent exception to the rule, but as Xenophon's account of the matter shows, the real [heart] of the charge against Socrates was that, of his pupils, Alcibiades had done more than any other one man to ruin Athens in the recent war, and Critias had been the ruthless ringleader of the Thirty who had massacred thousands of Athenians a few years before. . . .

Democrats in general approved of the egalitarian principle. Demosthenes in one passage argues that what makes all citizens public spirited and generous is "that in a democracy each man considers that he himself has a share in equality and justice," and in another praises a law forbidding legislation directed against individuals as being good democratic doctrine, "for as everyone has an equal share in the rest of the constitution, so everyone is entitled to an equal share in the laws." The Athenians were not, however, either in theory or in practice, absolute egalitarians, but drew a distinction between different political functions. On one point they admitted no compromise —equality before the law; as Pericles says, "in their private disputes all share equality according to the laws." This to us elementary principle needed emphasis, for Plato's friends in the Thirty, when they drew up a new constitution, ordained that only the 3,000 full citizens were entitled to a legal trial and that all others might be summarily executed by order of the government. It was secured in the Athenian constitution not only by the right of every citizen to seek redress in the courts, but by the character of the courts which consisted of large juries drawn by lot from the whole body of the citizens.

The Athenians also attached great importance to the equality of all citizens in formulating and deciding public policy. This was secured by the right of every citizen to speak and vote in the Assembly, and by the composition of the Council of Five Hundred which prepared the agenda of the Assembly; this body was annually chosen by lot from all the [wards] of Attica. Here democratic principle came into conflict with the oligarchic view, developed at length by Plato, that government was an art, demanding the highest skill, and should therefore be entrusted to a select few. . . . [However], it was not "the rulers of the city" who were chosen by lot, but officials charged with limited routine duties for which little more than "a sense of decency and fair play" was required. Furthermore, it must be remembered that a magistrate had to pass a preliminary examination which was, it is true, usually formal but gave his enemies an opportunity for raking up his past; was liable to be deposed by a vote of the Assembly taken ten times a year; and after his year was subject to a scrutiny in which his accounts were audited and any citizen could charge him with inefficiency or abuse of authority. It is unlikely that many rogues or nincompoops would expose themselves to these risks. . . .

Plato also objects to state pay: "I am told," he says, "that Pericles made the Athenians idle and lazy and garrulous and avaricious by first putting them on state pay." This is an oft-repeated accusation but has very little substance. In a population which never sank below 20,000 adult males and probably reached twice that figure at its peak, the Council and the magistracies did not provide employment except on rare occasions; a man might not hold any magistracy more than once or sit on the Council more than twice in his life. Assemblies were held only on forty days in the year. It was only as a juror that a citizen could obtain more or less continuous employment, and here the rate of remuneration was so low—half a laborer's wage in the fifth century and a third in the late fourth, in fact little more than bare subsistence—that in the fifth century, if the picture drawn in Aristophanes' *Wasps* is true, it attracted only the elderly, past hard work, and in the early fourth century, when economic conditions were worse, according to Isocrates, the unemployed. . . .

It is more difficult to answer the question whether the Athenian democracy did or did not in fact exploit the rich for the benefit of the poor. In the distribution of political power and influence, the rich seem to have fared well. In the minor offices and on the Council and in the juries the poor no doubt predominated, though even here it would seem that by the fourth century the well-to-do were by no means crowded out. To the important military, diplomatic, and financial offices men of birth and wealth were generally elected. The orators who, normally holding no office, guided policy by their speeches in the Assembly were also mostly well-to-do, and many of them of good family. It was comparatively rarely that a self-made man . . . achieved political influence. A rich man or an aristocrat certainly did not find that his political career was prejudiced by his wealth or birth, while poor and humbly born politicians had to face a good deal of abuse from comedians and orators. . . .

The philosophers held that the state ought to mould and train the citizens in virtue, and assumed that the average man was naturally evil or at least foolish. Political power must therefore be given to a select group of wise good men, who would impose a good way of life on the rest by a rigid system of education and control. The Athenian democrats, on the other hand, took an optimistic view of human nature and believed that every citizen should be allowed to live his own life in his own way within the broad limits laid down by the law, and that all citizens could be trusted to take their part in the government of the city, whether by voting and speaking in the Assembly, judging in the juries, carrying on the routine administration as magistrates, or selecting the men to hold high political office. On one point the Athenians were distrustful of human nature, on its ability to resist the temptations of irresponsible power; hence their insistence on brief terms of office, regular review of the conduct of magistrates in office, and above all a searching scrutiny of the record of magistrates on completing their term. The philosophers are strangely blind to this danger and are content to rely on the virtue of their usually hereditary or co-optative oligarchies of wise men.

The ideals of the Athenian democracy are perhaps best summed up in a rather florid passage of the Funeral Oration attributed to Lysias. Our ancestors, he says, "were the first and only men of that time who cast out arbitrary power and established democracy, holding that the freedom of all was the greatest concord, and sharing with one another their hopes and perils they governed themselves with free hearts, honoring the good and chastising the bad by law. They held it bestial to constrain one another by force, and the part of men to define justice by law and to persuade by reason and serve both by action, having law as their king and reason as their teacher."

3

ALEXANDER THE GREAT
AND THE UNITY OF MANKIND

Whatever their virtues, the Greek city-states were hopelessly parochial in outlook. A fanatic obsession with autonomy at the municipal level isolated the cities from their neighbors and aborted attempts at federalism. Inherently divided, the Greeks were easily subdued by Philip II of Macedon. Like it or not, the cities were dragooned into his Hellenic League which subordinated local rivalries to a common aim (i.e. the supremacy of Macedon). In the name of the Hellenic League, Philip's son Alexander III conquered the Persian Empire, and the Greek cities suddenly became part of a vast international society. "Who could imagine fifty years ago the amazing world of today?" asked one awed philosopher. Politically, the Greek cities were either subjects or satellites of the national states which were established by Alexander's successors: the Ptolemies in Egypt, the Antigonids in Macedon, the Seleucids in Syria and Iraq, and later the Attalids in Asia Minor. The number of Greek cities expanded as settlements were founded throughout the Near East, and Alexandria in Egypt was the largest, most prosperous, and impressive city in the Hellenistic world. Culturally, Hellas extended from Marseilles to the Punjab, and a merchant or tourist from Sicily could feel somewhat at home visiting the Greek rajahs of the Indus valley. Hellenistic culture tended to overwhelm local art and literature, for intellectuals and social-climbers eagerly embraced Greek ways much as modern Asians and Africans adopt Western culture. A notable exception was the Maccabean movement in Palestine, but the Jews of the Diaspora (and indeed many Palestinian Jews) were highly Hellenized. The famous Septuagint translation of the Old Testament into Greek was a symptom of the overriding Hellenism of the age. Though the cities were no longer independent states, the mental horizons of their inhabitants were broadened—the Greek view of the world gained perspective, and many Greeks became cosmopolitan. However, the new attitude was not altruistic and humanitarian, for an awareness of others does not necessarily lead to love. Many of the Macedonian kings saw their non-Greek subjects, much as Kipling viewed the Indians, as useful taxpayers and servants but certainly not the equals of the Pukka Sahibs. Nevertheless, many Greek soldiers and businessmen married native women and produced a new breed of "Greeks," who were joined by the Hellenized intelligentsia and the citizens of Antioch and other new cities. Hellenistic art reflected the greater realism of the new age, and Hellenistic thought expressed a cosmopolitanism foreign to Pericles and Plato.

This broad new world with its sophistication and problems was created by Alexander, who had conquered it in a triumphal sweep through the Persian Empire. Born in 356 B.C., Alexander was the able son of an ambitious father, and he inherited Philip's plan to seize the Near East from the Persians. With Philip's hardy veterans and expert staff officers, Alexander carried out his father's aims and defeated the

Persian monarch Darius III by 331 B.C. Instead of merely holding the Near East, the young conqueror resolved to outdo his father and assumed the Persian throne. As King of Kings, Alexander openly sought the cooperation of the nobles of Persia. A compulsive adventurer, he also needed to outdo his Persian predecessors and embarked on the conquest of India. However, his exhausted troops refused to advance beyond the Punjab, and Alexander was forced to return to Mesopotamia. Frustrated by his failure in India and quarreling with his generals, Alexander succumbed to drink or poison and died in 323 B.C. Relations between the king and the Macedonians had been strained by his high-handed manner and his pro-Persian policies. The veterans did not appreciate it when Alexander adopted Persian dress and wanted courtiers to prostrate themselves before him. His claim to be the son of a god, Zeus-Ammon, probably offended the Zarathustrian Persians more than the polytheistic Macedonians and Greeks, but most men took it as the whim of an arrogant prince. However, Alexander's successors followed his precedent and utilized the concept of a god-king to bolster their military monarchies.

How great was Alexander? Unquestionably, he was a first-rate soldier, though much of his success was due to the superb military machine which Philip had forged, and the headstrong Alexander took unnecessary risks in battle. As King of Kings, he had sense enough to realize that he could not run his empire without the cooperation of the Persian aristocracy, and he astutely won their support by adopting Persian clothes and court protocol. The areas he conquered were immense, but so were the lands subdued by Genghis Khan, and the Mongols cleverly supported the religions of subject peoples. There have been few stupid successful conquerors in world history, but greatness is, or should be, a hallowed word. Caesar was a greater man than Alexander, and Socrates was greater than both of them. Not really a Greek, the Macedonian king imposed unity on the Near East in the name of Hellenism. Two other outsiders, the Corsican Bonaparte and the Austrian Hitler, imposed unity on Europe in the name of a supposedly superior culture, respectively that of France and Germany. The unity effected by all three conquerors was a fragile creation based on war and despotism, and the three empires shattered within a few years of their inceptions. Dante was not impressed by similar despots: "What mean their trumpets and their bells, their horns and their flutes, but 'Come, hangman—come, vultures!'?" In this sense, Alexander must be ranked among the spoilers of the earth. True, he was a man of ability and not a wholly destructive barbarian, but Alexander was not worthy of the title Great.

The personality of Alexander is well documented. The Macedonians were notorious as heavy drinkers. Even Philip was often drunk, and Alexander was a chip off the old block. The tradition favorable to Alexander concedes that he was overly fond of wine, and the hostile tradition depicts him as an alcoholic despot. In his cups, the king murdered a veteran officer, Cleitus, who had once saved his life in battle. Alexander's other crimes rarely were outbursts of drunken fury but were usually calculated political acts. In one purge, he killed the cavalry commander Philotas on a charge of treason and ordered the execution of Philotas's father Parmenion on general principles. Some of Alexander's victims were guilty of conspiring against the king, but others were struck down in far-reaching purges. Aristotle's tactless nephew Callisthenes was slain for criticizing the monarch. On occasion, the erratic Alexander released his anger by massacring luckless natives. One tradition attributes his death to poison administered by agents of the viceroy of Macedon, Philip's old friend Antipater, who was a bitter foe of Alexander's mother Olympias. A strong-willed emotional woman, she had poisoned her son with a more subtle venom years before. Jealous of Philip's infidelities, she engulfed Alexander in excessive maternal love and encouraged his boyish resentment of Philip's many accomplishments. Alexander's obsession to outdo Philip was the result of his mother's constant prompting. She also told her devoted son that the hated Philip was not really his father, but rather that he had been sired by a deity—thus, in later life Alexander insisted on being worshiped as the son of Zeus-Ammon. Antipater and the older officers were hardly pleased when Alexander claimed that Philip had been cuckolded by a god. Fearing that Philip might hand the throne to another son, Olympias had engineered the assassination of her husband, or so Antipater believed. As King of Kings, Alexander did not let his mother meddle in matters of high policy, but he also rebuffed Antipater's complaints of her constant intrigues. Even Alexander's admirer Tarn admits that "it is doubtful if he ever cared for any woman except his terrible mother." In essence, Alexander was a spoiled mamma's boy with a violent temper, paranoid traits, and a dependence on alcohol. On the other hand, he was, like Philip, politically astute and an able manipulator of men.

The meteoric career of Alexander had qualities of epic romance, and the Macedonian conqueror has been the subject of many legends. Alexander's image dazzled even Caesar in his sillier moments, and Napoleon struck an Alexandrine pose, strutting before the pyramids and boasting of a march on India. In the Middle Ages, both Christians and Muslims idolized the invincible Alexander as a hero of chivalry. Chaucer summarized the eternal image of Alexander:

The pryde of man and beste he layde adoun,
Wher-so he cam, unto the worldes ende.

In his own lifetime, Alexander aided the legendmongers by hiring Callisthenes as a public relations man. Callisthenes supplied Greek audiences with exaggerated tales of Alexander's prowess and divinity, but the publicist perished when the royal egomaniac began to believe the lies. In the twentieth century, Alexander has become the hero of a new myth. Sir William Tarn hailed him as an inspired prophet of world unity and the brotherhood of man:

There is certainly a line of descent from his prayer at Opis, through the Stoics and one portion of the Christian ideal, to that brotherhood of all men which was proclaimed, though only proclaimed, in the French Revolution. The torch Alexander lit for long only smouldered; perhaps it still only smoulders today, but it never has been, and never can be, quite put out.[1]

[1] Sir W. W. Tarn in *The Cambridge Ancient History* (Cambridge: Cambridge University Press, 1927), Vol. VI, p. 437.

Tarn's messianic Alexander has been widely accepted by modern readers who respond to the attractiveness of unity and brotherhood without inquiring into the validity of the notion that Alexander too believed in these commendable ideals. Once established, a myth is hard to shake (however easy it may be to refute), for a successful myth answers a deep need in its believers. Amid endless wars and mounting anxieties, we fear that life is a running sore and history a chamber of horrors. How comforting it would be if there had once been a brave young king who wanted to save mankind from its baser instincts and promote a reign of peace and justice; and if he had not been cut down in his prime, dead at the age of thirty-two, the messiah would have established the kingdom of God on earth. If only it were true. . . .

JUSTIN

ALEXANDER THE DESPOT

Like many American students, Roman readers were fond of oversimplified digests of complex subjects, such as science or history. A prime specimen of this instant education was the work of Justin, who composed a handy outline of history in the third or fourth century A.D. No scholar himself, Justin simply boiled down an earlier digest by Trogus Pompeius who had made a sketch of Greek history for hurried readers in the time of Augustus. At least Trogus consulted the major Greek historians, but filtered through Trogus and Justin we see them "through a glass darkly." One of the main traditions hostile to Alexander stemmed from the writings of the Peripatetic school, which took a dim view of the king who had executed Aristotle's nephew Callisthenes. Whatever his ultimate source (via Trogus), Justin depicts Alexander as a cruel, cunning despot.

Alexander assumed the attire of the Persian monarchs as well as the diadem, which was unknown to the kings of Macedonia, as if he gave himself up to the customs of those whom he had conquered. And lest such innovations should be viewed with dislike if adopted by himself alone, he desired his friends also to wear the long robe of gold and purple. That he might imitate the luxury too as well as the dress of the Persians, he spent his nights among troops of the king's concubines of eminent beauty and birth. To these extravagances he added vast magnificence in feasting; and lest his entertainments should seem jejune and parsimonious, he accompanied his banquets, according to the osten-

tation of the eastern monarchs, with games, being utterly unmindful that power is accustomed to be lost, not gained, by such practices.

During the course of these proceedings, there arose throughout the camp a general indignation that he had so degenerated from his father Philip as to abjure the very name of his country and to adopt the manners of the Persians whom . . . he had overcome. But that he might not appear to be the only person who yielded to the vices of those whom he had conquered in the field, he permitted his soldiers also, if they had formed a connection with any of the female captives, to marry them, thinking that

From Justin, XII, 3–7, 10–12, tr. John S. Watson, in *Justin, Cornelius Nepos, and Eutropius*, a volume in Bohn's Libraries (London, (1910), pp. 108–12, 115–17. Reprinted by permission of the publisher, G. Bell & Sons, Ltd.

they would feel less desire to return to their country when they had some appearance of a house and home in the camp and that the fatigues of war would be relieved by the agreeable society of their wives. He saw too that Macedonia would be less drained to supply the army if the sons as recruits should succeed their veteran fathers and serve within the ramparts within which they were born, and would be likely to show more courage if they passed not only their earliest days of service but also their infancy in the camp. This custom was also continued under Alexander's successors. Maintenance was provided for the boys, and arms and horses were given them when they grew up; and rewards were assigned to the fathers in proportion to the number of their children. If the fathers of any of them were killed, the orphans notwithstanding received their father's pay, and their childhood was a sort of military service in various expeditions. Inured from their earliest years to toils and dangers, they formed an invincible army; they looked upon their camp as their country and upon a battle as a prelude to victory.

Alexander, meanwhile, began to show a passionate temper towards those about him, not with a princely severity but with the vindictiveness of an enemy. What most incensed him was, that reflections were cast upon him in the common talk of the soldiers for having cast off the customs of his father Philip and of his country. For this offence, Parmenion, an old man next to the king in rank, and his son Philotas were put to death, an examination by torture having been previously held on both of them. At this instance of cruelty, all the soldiers throughout the camp began to express their displeasure, being concerned for the fate of the innocent old general and his son and saying at times that "they must expect nothing better for themselves." These murmurs coming to the knowledge of Alexander, he, fearing that such reports would be carried to Macedonia and that the glory of his victories would be sullied by the stain of cruelty, pretended that he was going to send home some of his friends to give an account of his successes. He exhorted his soldiers to write to their relatives as they would now have fewer opportunities on account of the scene of warfare being further from home. The packets of letters, as they were given in, he commanded to be privately brought to him, and having learned from them what everyone thought of him, he put all those, who had given unfavorable opinions of his conduct, into one regiment with an intention

either to destroy them or to distribute them in colonies in the most distant parts of the earth. . . .

He invited his friends on some particular day to a banquet where mention being made, when they were intoxicated, of the great things achieved by Philip, he began to prefer himself to his father and to extol the vastness of his own exploits to the skies, the greater part of the company agreeing with him; and when Clitus, one of the older guests, trusting to his hold on the king's friendship in which he held the principal place, defended the memory of Philip and praised his acts, he so provoked Alexander that he snatched a weapon from one of the guards and slew him with it in the midst of the guests. Exulting at the murder, too, he scoffed at the dead man for his defence of Philip and his commendation of his mode of warfare. But when his mind, satiated with the bloodshed, grew calm and reflection took the place of passion, he began . . . to feel the deepest sorrow for the deed, grieving that he had listened to his father's praises with more anger than he ought to have listened to insults on his memory, and that an old and blameless friend had been slain by him at a feast and carousal. Driven therefore to repentance with the same vehemence with which he had before been impelled to resentment, he determined to die. Bursting into tears, he embraced the dead man, laid his hand on his wounds, and confessed his madness to him as if he could hear; then, snatching up a weapon, he pointed it against his breast and would have committed suicide, had not his friends interposed. His resolution to die continued even for several days after. . . . He reflected . . . what remarks and odium he must have occasioned as well in his own army as among the conquered nations; what fear and dislike of himself among his other friends; and how dismal and sad he had rendered his entertainment, appearing not less to be dreaded at a feast than when armed in the field of battle. Parmenion and Philotas, his cousin Amyntas, his murdered stepmother and brothers, with Attalus, Eurylochus, Pausanias, and other slaughtered nobles of Macedonia presented themselves to his imagination. He in consequence persisted in abstaining from food for four days until he was drawn from his purpose by the prayers of the whole army, who conjured him "not to lament the death of one so far as to ruin them all, since, after bringing them into the remotest part of the barbarians' country, he would leave them amidst hostile nations exasperated by war." The entreaties of Callisthenes the philosopher had great effect upon him, a man who was intimate with him from having been his fellow-student under Aristotle and who had been subsequently sent for, by the king himself, to record his acts for the perusal of posterity.

Soon after, he gave orders that he should not be approached with mere salutation but with adoration, a point of Persian pride to which he had hesitated to advance at first, lest the assumption of everything at once should excite too strong a feeling against him. Among those who refused to obey, the most resolute was Callisthenes, but his opposition proved fatal both to himself and to several other eminent Macedonians, who were all put to death on the pretence that they were engaged in a conspiracy. The custom of saluting their king was however retained by the Macedonians, adoration being set aside. . . .

He married Statira, the daugher of King Darius [at Susa], but at the same time he gave the noblest virgins, chosen from all the conquered natives, as wives to the chiefs of the Macedonians, in order that the impropriety of the king's conduct might be rendered less glaring by the practice becoming general. He next assembled the army [at Opis] and promised that "he would pay all their debts at his own expense," so that they might carry home their spoil and prizes undiminished. . . . Discharging some of the veterans, he recruited the army with younger soldiers. But those that were retained, murmuring at the discharge of the older men, demanded that they themselves should be released likewise, desiring that "their years, not of life, but of service should be counted." . . . Nor did they address the king only with entreaties but also with reproaches, bidding him "carry on his wars alone with the aid of

his father Ammon, since he looked with disdain on his soldiers." Alexander, on the other hand, sometimes upbraided his men and sometimes charged them in gentle terms "not to tarnish their glorious services by mutiny." At last, when he could produce no effect by words, he leaped unarmed from his tribunal among the armed multitude to lay hands on the authors of the mutiny, and not a man daring to oppose him, he led thirteen of them . . . to punishment. Such submission to death did the fear of their king produce in the men. . . . He then addressed himself in a public speech to the auxiliary troops of the Persians apart from the Macedonians. He extolled their constant fidelity, as well as to himself as to their former kings; he mentioned the kindnesses which he had shown them, saying that "he had never treated them as a conquered people, but always as sharers in his successes; that he had gone over to the usages of their nation, not they to those of his; and that he had mingled the conquerors with the conquered by matrimonial connections. And now," he added, "he would entrust the guardianship of his person, not to the Macedonians only, but also to them." Accordingly, he enrolled a thousand of their young men among his bodyguard and at the same time incorporated into his army a portion of the auxiliaries trained after the discipline of the Macedonians. At this proceeding the Macedonians were much dissatisfied, exclaiming that "their enemies were put into their places by their king," and at length they all went to Alexander in a body, beseeching him with tears "to content himself rather with punishing than ill-treating them." By this modest forbearance they produced such an effect upon him that he released eleven thousand veterans more.

ARRIAN, ERATOSTHENES, PLUTARCH

ALEXANDER THE UNIFIER

The three following passages—a straightforward historical account, an inference of principle, and an exaggerated burst of rhetoric—have been used to justify the image of Alexander the unifier. The best extant life of Alexander was written in the second century A.D. by Arrian, who used the memoirs of the engineer Aristobulus and King Ptolemy I of Egypt. Eratosthenes was a famous polymath, literary critic, and scientist of the third century B.C. He served as Director of the great Alexandrian Library and is best known for his remarkably accurate estimate of the size of the earth. Plutarch was a Greek moralist and essayist of the late first and early second century A.D. His essay on the "Fortune of Alexander" was a youthful exercise in rhetoric and not a balanced historical estimate of the effect of Alexander on the East. In later life, Plutarch wrote a biography of Alexander which shows the king in a less favorable light.

1. ARRIAN

[Arrian has just described the suppression of the mutiny at Opis and Alexander's demonstration of favor toward the Persian soldiery. The Macedonians were shocked by the new policy.] When the news was reported to them about the Persians and Medes, . . . they were no longer able to restrain themselves, but running in a body to the palace, they cast their weapons there in front of the gates as signs of supplication to the king. . . . At length one of them, Callines by name, a man conspicuous both for his age and because he was a captain of the Companion cavalry, spoke as follows: "O king, what grieves the Macedonians is that you have already made some of the Persians kinsmen to yourself, and that Persians are called Alexander's kinsmen and have the honor of saluting you with a kiss, whereas none of the Macedonians has as yet enjoyed this honor." Then Alexander interrupting him, said: "But all of you without exception I consider my kinsmen, and so from this time I shall call you." When he had said this, Callines advanced and saluted him with a kiss, and so did all those who wished to salute him. Then they took up their weapons and returned to the camp, shouting and singing a song of thanksgiving. After this Alexander offered sacrifice to the gods to whom it was his custom to sacrifice, and gave a public banquet over which he himself presided, with the Macedonians sitting around him and next to them the Persians, after whom came the men of the other nations, preferred in honor for their personal rank or for some meritorious action. The king and his guests drew wine from the same bowl and poured out the same libations, both the Grecian prophets and the Magians commencing the ceremony. He prayed for other blessings and especially that harmony and community of rule might exist between the Macedonians and Persians. The common account is, that those who took part in this banquet were 9,000 in number, that all of them poured out one libation, and after it sang a song of thanksgiving. Then those of the Macedonians who were unfit for service on account of age or any other misfortune went back [to Macedon] of their own accord, to the number of about 10,000.

2. ERATOSTHENES

[The geographer Strabo makes a parenthetical remark on Eratosthenes' view of Alexander]: Towards the end of his treatise—after withholding praise from those who divide the whole multitude of mankind into two groups, namely Greeks and barbarians, and also from those who advised Alexander to treat the Greeks as friends but the barbarians as enemies—Eratosthenes goes on to say that it would be better to make such divisions according to good qualities and bad qualities, for not only are many of the Greeks bad, but many of the barbarians are refined—Indians and [Iranians] for example, and further, Romans and Carthaginians who carry on their governments so admirably. And this, he says, is the reason why Alexander, disregarding his advisers, welcomed as many as he could of the men of fair repute and did them favors.

3. PLUTARCH

[Plutarch is arguing that Alexander was really a philosopher in action]: Compare Alexander's pupils

From Arrian, "Anabasis of Alexander," VII, 11–12, tr. Edward J. Chinnock, in *The Greek Historians,* edited by Francis R. B. Godolphin, Vol. II, pp. 601–2. Copyright 1942 by Random House, Inc. Reprinted by permission.

From Strabo, I 4.9. Reprinted by permission of the publishers and the Loeb Classical Library from Horace L. Jones, *The Geography of Strabo* (Cambridge, Mass.: Harvard University Press, 1960; London: William Heinemann Ltd.), pp. 247–49.

From Plutarch, "The Fortune of Alexander," 328B–329D, 330A, C–E. Reprinted by permission of the publishers and the Loeb Classical Library from *Plutarch's Moralia,* tr. Frank C. Babbitt (Cambridge, Mass.: Harvard University Press, 1936; London: William Heinemann Ltd.), Vol. IV, pp. 393–99, 403, 405.

with those of Plato and Socrates. Plato and Socrates taught pupils of splendid natural endowment who spoke the same language, so that, even if the pupils understood nothing else, at least they understood the Greek tongue. And even so, Plato and Socrates did not win over many. But their pupils, such as Critias and Alcibiades . . . , were prone to spew the good word forth, as a horse the curbing bit, and turned them to other ways. But if you examine the results of Alexander's instruction, you will see that he educated the Hyrcanians to respect the marriage bond and taught the Arachosians to till the soil and persuaded the Sogdians to support their parents, not to kill them, and the Persians to revere their mothers and not to take them in wedlock. O wondrous power of Philosophic Instruction that brought the Indians to worship Greek gods and the Scythians to bury their dead, not to devour them! We admire Carneades' power which made Cleitomachus, formerly called Hasdrubal and a Carthaginian by birth, adopt Greek ways. We admire the character of Zeno which persuaded Diogenes the Babylonian to be a philosopher. But when Alexander was civilizing Asia, Homer was commonly read, and the children of the Persians [etc.] learned to chant the tragedies of Sophocles and Euripides. And although Socrates, when tried on the charge of introducing foreign deities, lost his cause to the informers who infested Athens, yet through Alexander, Bactria and the Caucasus learned to revere the gods of the Greeks. Plato wrote a book on the one ideal constitution, but because of its forbidding character he could not persuade anyone to adopt it, but Alexander established more than seventy cities among savage tribes and sowed all Asia with Grecian magistracies and thus overcame its uncivilized and brutish manner of living. Although few of us read Plato's Laws, yet hundreds of thousands have made use of Alexander's laws and continue to use them. Those who were vanquished by Alexander are happier than those who escaped his hand. . . . Alexander's new subjects would not have been civilized had they not been vanquished: Egypt would not have its Alexandria, nor Mesopotamia its Seleuceia, nor Sogdiana its Prophthasia, nor India its Bucephalia, nor the Caucasus a Greek city hard by; for by the founding of cities in these places, savagery was extinguished and the worse element, gaining familiarity with the better, changed under its influence. If then philosophers take the greatest pride in civilizing and rendering adaptable the intractable and untutored elements in human character, and if Alexander has been shown to have changed the savage natures of

countless tribes, it is with good reason that he should be regarded as a very great philosopher.

Moreover, the much-admired *Republic* of Zeno, the founder of the Stoic sect, may be summed up in this one main principle: that all the inhabitants of this world of ours should not live differentiated by their respective rules of justice into separate cities and communities, but that we should consider all men to be of one community and one polity, and that we should have a common life and an order common to us all, even as a herd that feeds together and shares the pasturage of a common field. This Zeno wrote, giving shape to a dream or, as it were, shadowy picture of a well-ordered and philosophic commonwealth, but it was Alexander who gave effect to the idea. For Alexander did not follow Aristotle's advice to treat the Greeks as if he were their leader, and other peoples as if he were their master; to have regard for the Greeks as for friends and kindred, but to conduct himself toward other peoples as though they were plants or animals; for to do so would have been to cumber his leadership with numerous battles and banishments and festering seditions. But, as he believed that he came as a heaven-sent governor to all and as a mediator for the whole world, those whom he could not persuade to unite with him, he conquered by force of arms, and he brought together into one body all men everywhere, uniting and mixing in one great loving-cup, as it were, men's lives, their characters, their marriages, their very habits of life. He bade them all consider as their fatherland the whole inhabited earth, as their stronghold and protection his camp, as akin to them all good men, and as foreigners only the wicked. They should not distinguish between Grecian and foreigner by Grecian cloak and [shield] or scimitar and jacket, but the distinguishing mark of the Grecian should be seen in virtue and that of the foreigner in iniquity; clothing and food, marriage and manner of life they should regard as common to all, being blended into one by ties of blood and children. . . .

As sovereign of both nations and benevolent king, he strove to acquire the goodwill of the conquered by showing respect for their apparel, so that they might continue constant in loving the Macedonians as rulers and might not feel hate toward them as enemies. . . . Although paying due respect to his own national dress, he did not disdain that of his conquered subjects in establishing the beginnings of a vast empire. For he did not overrun Asia like a robber nor was he minded to tear and rend it, as if it were booty and plunder bestowed by unexpected good fortune. . . . Alexander desired to render all upon earth subject to one law of reason and one form of government and to reveal all men as one people, and to this purpose he made himself conform. But if the deity that sent down Alexander's soul into this world of ours had not recalled him quickly, one law would govern all mankind and they all would look toward one rule of justice as though toward a common source of light. But, as it is, that part of the world which has not looked upon Alexander has remained without sunlight.

WILLIAM W. TARN

ALEXANDER THE DREAMER

The late Sir William W. Tarn (1869-1957) was a scholar with vast learning and a vivid imagination. He was renowned for his study of *Alexander the Great* (1948), an excellent textbook *Hellenistic Civilization* (1927), and the chapters which he contributed to the monumental *Cambridge Ancient History*. More than any single individual, Tarn made the English-speaking world aware of the vitality and importance of the Hellenistic Age. His scholarly attainments are unquestioned, but he felt strongly about individuals in the past and his enthusiasm often overcame his common sense. Tarn's vision of Alexander as an apostle of "one world" and brotherly love was a noble dream which has influenced many writers and is still popular in some quarters. In 1933 Tarn delivered the Raleigh Lecture on History before the British Academy; his topic was "Alexander the Great and the Unity of Mankind."

What I am going to talk about is one of the great revolutions in human thought. Greeks of the classical period, speaking very roughly, divided mankind into two classes, Greeks and non-Greeks; the latter they called barbarians and usually regarded as inferior people, though occasionally some one, like Herodotus or Xenophon, might suggest that certain barbarians possessed qualities which deserved consideration, like the wisdom of the Egyptians or the courage of the Persians. But in the third century B.C. and later we meet with a body of opinion which may be called universalist; all mankind was one and all men were brothers, or anyhow ought to be. Who was the pioneer who brought about this tremendous revolution in some men's way of thinking? Most writers have had no doubt on that point; the man to whom the credit was due was Zeno, the founder of the Stoic philosophy. But there are several passages in Greek writers which, *if* they are to be believed, show that the first man actually to think of it was not Zeno but Alexander. This matter has never really been examined; some writers just pass it over, which means, I suppose, that they do not consider the passages in question historical; others have definitely said that it is merely a case of our secondary authorities attributing to Alexander ideas taken from Stoicism. I want to consider today whether the passages in question are or are not historical and worthy of credence; that is, whether Alexander was or was not the first to believe in, and to contemplate, the unity of mankind. This will entail among other things some examination of the concept which Greeks called Homonoia, a word which meant more than its Latin translation, Concord, means to us; it is more like Unity and Concord, a being of one mind together, or if we like the phrase, a union of hearts; ultimately it was to become almost a symbol of the world's

From William W. Tarn, "Alexander the Great and the Unity of Mankind," *Proceedings of the British Academy*, XIX (1933), pp. 123–27, 145–48.

longing for something better than constant war. For convenience of discussion, I shall keep the Greek term Homonoia. . . .

The Greek world, whatever its practice, never doubted that in theory unity in a city was very desirable, but though the word Homonoia was already in common use among Greeks, it chiefly meant absence of faction-fights, and this rather negative meaning lasted in the cities throughout the Hellenistic period, as can be seen in the numerous decrees in honor of the judicial commissions sent from one city to another, which are praised because they tried to compose internal discord. There was hardly a trace as yet of the more positive sense which Homonoia was to acquire later—a mental attitude which should make war or faction impossible because the parties were at one; and Isocrates extended the application of the word without changing its meaning. He took up a suggestion of the sophist Gorgias and proposed to treat the whole Greek world as one and the futile wars between city and city as faction fights—to apply Homonoia to the Greek race. For this purpose he utilized Plato's idea that the barbarian was a natural enemy, and decided that the way to unite Greeks was to attack Persia; "I come," he said, "to advocate two things: war against the barbarian, Homonoia between ourselves." But somebody had to do the uniting; and Isocrates bethought him of the Cynic Heracles, benefactor of the Greek race, and urged King Philip of Macedonia, a descendant of Heracles, to play the part. But if Philip was to be Heracles and bring about the Homonoia of the Greek world, the way was being prepared for two important ideas of a later time; the essential quality of the king must be that love of man . . . which had led Heracles to perform his labors, and the essential business of the king was to promote Homonoia; so far this only applied to Greeks, but if its meaning were to deepen, it would still be the king's business. The actual result of all this, the League of Corinth under Philip's presidency, was not quite what Isocrates had dreamt of.

This then was the background against which Alexander appeared. The business of a Macedonian king was to be a benefactor of Greeks to the extent of preventing inter-city warfare; he was to promote Homonoia among Greeks and utilize their enmity to barbarians as a bond of union; but barbarians themselves were still enemies and slaves by nature, a view which Aristotle emphasized when he advised his pupil to treat Greeks as free men but barbarians as slaves.

I now come to the things Alexander is supposed to have said or thought, and the gulf between them and the background I have sketched is so deep that one cannot blame those who have refused to believe that he ever said or thought anything of the sort. There are five passages which need consideration: one in Arrian; one from Eratosthenes, preserved by Strabo; and three from Plutarch, one of which, from its resemblance to the Strabo passage, has been supposed by one of the acutest critics of our time to be taken in substance from Eratosthenes, and as such I shall treat it. The passage in Arrian says that, after the mutiny of the Macedonians at Opis and their reconciliation to Alexander, he gave a banquet to Macedonians and Persians, at which he prayed for Homonoia and partnership in rule between these two peoples. What Eratosthenes says amounts to this. Aristotle told Alexander to treat Greeks as friends but barbarians like animals; but Alexander knew better and preferred to divide men into good and bad without regard to their race. . . . For Alexander believed that he had a mission from the deity to harmonize men generally and be the reconciler of the world, mixing men's lives and customs as in a loving cup, and treating the good as his kin, the bad as strangers; for he thought that the good man was the real Greek and the bad man the real barbarian. Of the two Plutarch passages, the first says that his intention was to bring about, as between mankind generally, Homonoia and peace and fellowship and make them all one people; and the other, which for the moment I will quote without its context, makes him say that God is the common father of all men.[1]

It is obvious that, wherever all this comes from, we are dealing with a great revolution in thought. It amounts to this, that there is a natural brotherhood of all men, though bad men do not share in it; that Homonoia is no longer to be confined to the relations between Greek and Greek, but is to unite Greek and barbarian; and that Alexander's aim was to substitute peace for war and reconcile the enmities of mankind by bringing them all—all that is whom his arm could reach, the peoples of his empire—to be of one mind together: as men were one in blood, so

---

[1] Plutarch, *Alexander* 27: "He said that God was a common father of us all, but especially of the best of us." The context is the episode at Siwah when the oracle hailed Alexander as the son of the god Zeus-Ammon. [Editor's note.]

they should become one in heart and spirit. That such a revolution in thought did happen is unquestioned; the question is, was Alexander really its author, or are the thoughts attributed to him those of Zeno or somebody else? . . . Plutarch says that behind Zeno's dream lay Alexander's reality, and no one doubts that Alexander was Zeno's inspiration, but the question is, in what form? Most writers have taken Plutarch to mean Alexander's empire, but to me this explains nothing at all. . . . It does seem to me that what Plutarch really means is not Alexander's empire but Alexander's ideas; after all, the frequent references in antiquity to Alexander as a philosopher, one at least of which is contemporary, must mean *something*. Zeno's inspiration, then, was Alexander's idea of the unity of mankind, and what Zeno himself did was to carry this idea to one of its two logical conclusions. Judging by his prayer at Opis for the Homonoia of Macedonians and Persians, Alexander, had he lived, would have worked through national groups, as was inevitable in an empire like his, which comprised many different states and subject peoples. . . . But Zeno abolished all distinctions of race, all the apparatus of national groups and particular states, and made his world-state a theoretic whole. . . . Alexander's way, or what I think was his way, led to the Roman empire being called one people. . . .

Only one conclusion from all this seems possible: the things which, in the tradition, Alexander is supposed to have thought and said are, in substance, true. He did say that all men were sons of God, that is brothers, but that God made the best ones peculiarly his own; he did aspire to be the harmonizer and reconciler of the world—that part of the world which his arm reached; he did have the intention of uniting the peoples of his empire in fellowship and concord and making them of one mind together; and when, as a beginning, he prayed at Opis for partnership in rule and Homonoia between Macedonians and Persians, he meant what he said—not partnership in rule only, but true unity between them. I am only talking of theory, not of actions; but what this means is that he was the pioneer of one of the supreme revolutions in the world's outlook, the first man known to us who contemplated the brotherhood of man or the unity of mankind, whichever phrase we like to use. I do not claim to have given you exact proof of this; it is one of those difficult borderlands of history where one does not get proofs which could be put to a jury. But there is a very strong presumption indeed that it is true. Alexander, for the things he *did*, was called the Great; but if what I have said today be right, I do not think we shall doubt that this idea of his—call it a purpose, call it a dream, call it what you will —was the greatest thing about him.

ARNOLD J. TOYNBEE

THE ARCHANGEL ALEXANDER

Probably the most famous historian in the modern world is Arnold J. Toynbee of the Royal Institute of International Affairs. Though a classical scholar of considerable stature, he is most renowned for his twelve-volume *A Study of History* (1934– 1962) which in one form or another, usually in digest, has reached a wide audience. Essentially, Toynbee claims to understand the mechanics of the rise and fall of civilizations and he insists that the real function of a major society is the production of a "higher religion." Personally he is a man of charm, sincerity, and inherent goodness. At heart a poet and at times a mystic, Toynbee writes in a florid style which reflects the phraseology of the King James Bible. His persuasive style and religious tone have endeared his books to readers who are repelled by the grim pessimism of Spengler. However, Toynbee, like Spengler, has been unanimously condemned by competent historians who resent his pose of scientific objectivity and his cavalier distortions of fact. Heavily indebted to the ideas of Carl Jung, Toynbee is a meta-historian like Hegel[1] and his views are most impressive to those who are ignorant of the multiplicity and complexity of history. The Toynbee fad is a symptom of a time, and *A Study of History* will probably not survive the anxiety-ridden generation which has sought truth in its crowded pages. Needless to say, Tarn's vision of Alexander the dreamer struck a responsive note for Toynbee, the poet of history.

We children of the Western Society in the present generation are aware from our own experience how poignant this longing may be in an age when the unity of Mankind is being striven for unavailingly. In our day the universal state for which we yearn —the ecumenical commonwealth that will establish its peace from end to end of a Westernized and, by the same token, tormented world—has not yet made its epiphany even on the horizon; yet, in anticipation of its coming, its style and title—"the Great Society" —has been coined by a twentieth-century English sociologist [Graham Wallas] as a Western equivalent for the Hellenic "Inhabited World" and for the Sinic "All that is under Heaven."

It is this great longing for Peace on Earth after the tribulation of a "Time of Troubles" that has moved the subjects of the founders or preservers of the universal states to venerate them as Saviors of Society or actually to worship them as gods incarnate. And even the historian's colder judgment will single out as the greatest of all men of action those ecumenical rulers—a Cyrus, an Alexander, an Augustus—who have been touched with pity for the sufferings of their fellow men and, having caught the vision of the unity of Mankind, have devoted their personal genius and their political power to the noble enterprise of translating this dearly bought ideal into a humane reality.

Alexander's vision of Homonoia or Concord never faded out of the Hellenic World so long as a vestige of Hellenism remained in existence; and the compelling spiritual power of his humanitarian gospel is impressive in view of the recalcitrance of his Macedonian companions towards his efforts to induce them to fraternize with their defeated Iranian antagonists, and the equally stubborn recalcitrance of the rest of the Greeks towards his ordinance that the ruling faction in every city-state should reopen the gates to their exiled opponents of the contrary party.

All but a few of the Macedonian officers whom their royal leader had cajoled or dragooned into embarking with him on the pacific adventure of taking in marriage an Iranian bride might brutally repudiate their unwanted Oriental wives as soon as Alexander had been laid in his premature grave. Yet, some three hundred years after Alexander's death, we find Caesar Augustus putting Alexander's head on his Roman signet-ring as an acknowledgement of the source from which he was seeking inspiration for his arduous work of bringing a tardy peace and unity to a Hellenic World which Alexander's successors had thrown back into disunion and discord; and some two hundred years after Augustus' time, again, this Alexandrine tradition of humanitarianism still had power to move so coarse-grained and brutal a soul as Caracalla's to complete the process—which Julius Caesar had lavishly begun and Augustus cautiously continued—of conferring the Roman citizenship upon the subject majority in the population of the Roman empire.[2] Nor did Alexander's example merely influence the action of these later ecumenical rulers who sat in Alexander's seat and caught from that eminence Alexander's bird's-eye view of all his fellow men; the leaven also worked its way down through the variegated strata of a Hellenic Society which had now annexed the children of four submerged alien worlds to the Hellenic internal proletariat. It was Alexander's spirit that moved one Roman centurion at Capernaum to make his humble appeal to Jesus to heal his servant by simply speaking the word without coming under his roof, and that emboldened another Roman centurion at Caesarea to invite Peter to his house. It was Alexander's spirit, likewise, that inspired the Greeks who had come up to Jerusalem in order to worship at the feast to ask the disciples of Jesus whether their Master would grant them an audience; and we may believe that the same Alexandrine

[2]The emperor Caracalla extended citizenship in order to increase the revenue on certain taxes which only Roman citizens paid. A paranoid despot, he fancied that he was Alexander reborn and was murdered while marching against Persia. [Editor's note.]

[1]See Thomas W. Africa, "The City of God Revisited," *Journal of the History of Ideas*, XXIII (1962), pp. 281–292.

From Arnold J. Toynbee, *A Study of History* (London, 1939), Vol. VI, pp. 6–11. Published by the Oxford University Press under the auspices of the Royal Institute of International Affairs and reprinted by permission.

vision of the unity of Mankind was the human in-spiration in the mind of Jesus himself when he broke out into a paean of exultation upon learning of the Greeks' request, and again when, in his encounters with the dissident woman of Samaria and with the Hellenized woman of Phoenicia, he broke away from an inhuman Jewish tradition of non-intercourse with unbelievers.

If we are convinced that Alexander's gospel of the unity of Mankind did indeed possess this power of creating concord between souls so far removed in time and creed and class from the Macedonian warrior-visionary, then we shall find ourselves im-pelled to search for the source from which this extraordinary power was derived; and, if we address our inquiry in the first instance to a humanist of the modern Western school, he will probably reply that the Brotherhood of Man is one of those fundamental truths which, once seen, are recognized, in the same flash, as being self-evident; and he will be likely to add that the duty and desire to serve Humanity re-quire no sanctions outside themselves in any human heart that has become sensitively aware of its kinship with all its fellows. . . . The validity of the principle of Altruism is taken for granted by modern Western humanists of every sect. The Communist, for instance, believes, as devoutly as the Positivist, that Man's ultimate duty is owed to his fellow men in a Universe in which Humanity is monarch of all it surveys, because Man has no God above him; and yet we have seen reasons for believing that the dynamic elements in Communism—the springs of the action that has made Communism a force in contemporary human affairs—are derived, albeit unconsciously, from a trinity of theistic religions, if we are right in tracing back some of these elements to Christianity and others to Christianity's two forerunners, Judaism and Zoroastrianism. If we now return to our inquiry into the basis of the Humanism of Alexander, shall we find the theistic vein that is latent in Marx's Humanism anticipated in Alexander's vision?

There was, we must allow, in Alexander's life one arresting experience on the ordinary human plane which might have been sufficient in and by itself to open Alexander's eyes to the intellectual falsity and the moral indefensibility of the current Hellenic dichotomy of Mankind into "Hellenes" and "Bar-barians"; and that was his sensational discovery of the unexpected virtues of his defeated Iranian adver-saries. In the hostile caricature which had been the convention in Hellas during the interval of 146

years by which Alexander's passage of the Helles-pont was separated from Xerxes' unluckier crossing of the same straits in the opposite direction, the Persian grandees had been held up to odium as monsters of luxury, tyranny, cruelty, and cowardice; and now, when Xerxes' abortive aggression had been avenged at last up to the hilt by Alexander's victor-ious "retaliation," the Macedonian champion of Hellas learnt through the intimate and illuminating intercourse of warfare that these arch-barbarians were in reality men capable of showing a bravery in battle and a dignity in defeat which even a Spartan might envy. The deepness of the impression which this unlooked-for discovery made upon Alexander's mind is notorious; but if we go on to ask whether in Alexander's opinion this experience of his own or others like it would suffice in themselves to awaken in human souls a consciousness of the unity of Man-kind and a will to act upon this great discovery, our evidence (scanty though it is) will inform us explicitly that the answer is in this case in the negative. It is recorded that at Opis in Babylonia, Alexander once offered up a prayer that his Macedonians and his Persians might be united in Homonoia; and Plutarch reports as one of Alexander's sayings: "God is the common father of all men, but he makes the best ones peculiarly his own." If this "saying" is authentic, it tells us that Alexander's anthropology differed from that of Marx in the fundamental point of resting on an avowed theological foundation instead of professedly hanging in the air. It tells us that Alexander discovered the truth that the brother-hood of Man presupposes the fatherhood of God—a truth which involves the converse proposition that, if the divine father of the human family is ever left out of the reckoning, there is no possibility of forging any alternative bond of purely human texture which will avail by itself to hold Mankind together. The only society that is capable of embracing the whole of Mankind is a superhuman "City of God." . . . "Except the Lord build the house, their labor is but lost that build it; except the Lord keep the city, the watchman watcheth but in vain." The common experience of the Hellenic "Time of Troubles" taught this truth to Alexander the Greek and to Paul the Jew, . . . but the Hellenic Society has not been singular either in passing through great tribulation or in learning this lesson by suffering this affliction. In the Egyptiac World, more than a thousand years before Alexander made his pilgrimage to the oasis-oracle of Amon, the unity of Mankind was numbered among the mighty works of the divinity, manifested in the Sun-Disk, who was worshipped by Ikhnaton.

The Archangel Alexander

ERNST BADIAN

A CRITICAL APPRAISAL OF THE TARN THESIS

Professor Ernst Badian of the University of Leeds is highly regarded for his penetrating studies of Greek and Roman history. He is the author of *Foreign Clientelae* (1958), and a number of his essays were published in a collection in 1964. A pupil of Sir Ronald Syme, Badian is representative of the approach of many British scholars to antiquity. Paricularly since the Second World War, students of the Greek and Roman past have been noticeably drawn to a realistic solution to the complex problems of history. Though he can write with wit, Badian is engaged in the following passages with a straightforward critical appraisal of the Tarn thesis. Most of the quotations from Tarn are from his 1948 book on Alexander.

Twenty-five years ago Sir William Tarn delivered a Raleigh Lecture on History to the British Academy, to which he gave this challenging title [Alexander the Great and the Unity of Mankind] and in which he created the figure we may call Alexander the Dreamer: an Alexander "dreaming" of "one of the supreme revolutions in the world's outlook," namely "the brotherhood of man or the unity of mankind." . . . Six years later Tarn could write: "It is now, as I see it, certain." Ten years ago, in his great work on Alexander, certainty was apparently a little abated. But if there was less pretension, there was no more ability to think himself mistaken, and no more civility in dealing with opposing views. . . . Ever since 1933, Tarn's figure of Alexander the Dreamer . . . has haunted the pages of scholarship, and even source-books and general histories of philosophy and of ideas—at least in this country —have begun to succumb to the spell. Perhaps a quarter of a century is long enough for the life-span of a phantom: it is clearly threatening to pass into our tradition as a thing of flesh and blood. . . .

According to Tarn, Alexander developed "an idea which had three facets or aspects: . . . The first is that God is the common Father of mankind, which may be called the brotherhood of man. The second is Alexander's dream of the various races of mankind, so far as known to him, becoming of one mind together and living in unity and concord, which may be called the unity of mankind. And the third . . . is that the various peoples of his empire might be partners in the realm rather than subjects." Let us examine these "facets" in turn.

The first is not logically relevant to the other two: it is only by playing with imagery that we arrive from the idea of God as "the common Father of mankind" at that of the "brotherhood of man" in any ethically important sense. In fact, for reasons that nowadays need hardly be set out at length, the idea of God as "the common Father of mankind" is ethically neutral. On it, or on similar foundations, equalitarian and universalist ethics have in fact been founded—but also systems of chosen peoples, of lawful slavery, and all the class and race distinctions with which we are so familiar. To keep within the bounds of the image: God may still have all manner of favorite children, usually including the exponent of the theory advanced. This seems so elementary as to be hardly worth stressing. Yet it seems to have escaped Tarn's notice, as is clear from his exposition. Citing from Plutarch the report that Alexander "said that God was the common father of all mankind, but that he made the best ones peculiarly his own," he comments: "This, on the face of it, is a plain statement that all men are brothers." (And he goes on to say that it is the first.) On the face of it, it is hard not to see in it something quite different. Nor does scrutiny belie the first impression. Plutarch has been talking about Alexander's visit to Ammon and telling some of the stories that collected round

From Ernst Badian, "Alexander the Great and the Unity of Mankind," *Historia*, VII (1958), pp. 425–30, 432–33, 435–36. Reprinted by permission of Franz Steiner Verlag, publishers of *Historia*.

the oracle's replies to him; in particular, he has stressed the revelation to Alexander that he was to regard Zeus-Ammon as his father. . . . The story as Plutarch tells it . . . is not intended to, and it does not in the least, portray Alexander as believing in the brotherhood of man in any sense in which Greeks, ever since Homer, had not. . . . It is indeed surprising that such an elaborate house of cards should be built on a distortion of a reported saying. . . .

The other two "facets"—far more important—are fashioned out of the Opis banquet. . . . The scene is reported only by Arrian. . . . It is clear that to Arrian (i.e. to his source) the whole affair is not of outstanding importance. It is a tailpiece of merely two sections to the Opis mutiny, which *is* an important event . . . and it is immediately followed by the dismissal of the Macedonian veterans. This had been planned and announced before the mutiny and had been immediately responsible for its outbreak; and after its settlement it could at last be executed. The banquet, as we can see, just like the sacrifice that precedes it, marks the formal settlement of the dispute that had led to the mutiny; and it follows upon the account of the details of that settlement. The mutiny, as we are repeatedly and unanimously told, was due to the Macedonians' jealousy of the favor Alexander was showing to the "Persians." The reconciliation, therefore, might be expected to be between (a) Alexander and the Macedonians, whose quarrel *was* the mutiny; (b) the Macedonians and the "Persians," whose differences had caused it. . . . That the banquet marked "a greater reconciliation" or even the official conclusion of peace is neither stated nor implied in the source.

Tarn's scene-setting is at once splendid and misleading: . . . "No witness of the scene could ever have forgotten the sight of that great krater on Alexander's table and people of every nationality drawing wine from it for their common libation." It is a fit setting for a ceremony of international brotherhood. What, in fact, does Arrian (and we must agree with Tarn that that means Ptolemy) say? There is nothing about tables—how many were used and who used them—and certainly nothing about Alexander's own table; there is merely the statement that everyone was seated: apart from other reasons that might plausibly be conjectured, there were presumably too many people for everyone to be able to recline. Even a large refectory table could hardly have accommodated the crowd that Tarn wishes to place at

it. The source merely tells us how the guests were grouped within the area given over to the banquet—there is no implication that each group had only one table, and indeed numbers make it impossible. If Alexander had a table to share, he presumably shared it, on this occasion as on others, with a handful of high-ranking officers and courtiers.

On the *grouping*, however, the source is precise: around Alexander were Macedonians, next to them in order "Persians," next to them the rest. Thus, when "those around" Alexander join him in the libation from his krater, the emphatic repetition of the same phrase within a few words makes it clear that only the Macedonians are meant. No doubt the "Persians" and the rest poured the "same" libation—in an extended sense—from their own bowls: Arrian goes on to tell us that it is said 9000 people did so. But the sharing of Alexander's own krater was limited to the Macedonians. The inspiring ceremonial of an international love-feast is purely imaginary and due to misinterpretation of an unusually precise source. In fact, . . . treatment is carefully graded according to nationality—so far is it from being equal and cosmopolitan. . . . This fits in with what we have seen to be the purpose of the banquet and with the account of the mutiny and its settlement. Eager to regain the loyalty of his Macedonians (who were still his best soldiers and would be needed for his further plans of conquest), Alexander had called them "kinsmen" and thus made them—every common soldier of them—equal to the noblest of the "Persians." For he could be sure of the latter and their submissiveness, while the Macedonians had to be courted. He now reinforced this timely act of flattery by seating them "around him" at the banquet and letting them, and them only, use his own krater for the libation. After the banquet, of course, he proceeded to carry out his plans precisely as he had made them before the mutiny, and there was now no further protest: tact meant no surrender of principle. But the flamboyant gesture—as always, carefully calculated for political effect—reveals the unmistakable Alexander of history, who did not gain his empire by well-meaning muddle-headedness. The setting, then, is not that of an international love-feast. . . .

There is another passage in which Tarn seeks corroboration for his theory and in particular for his views on the Opis banquet: he claims the explicit support of Eratosthenes. Now Eratosthenes, of course, was far from being a contemporary of Alexander—so far that he could not even know any of his contemporaries; and though we admire him as a great scientist and mathematician, we have no means of assessing him as a historian or judging his skill in weighing historical evidence. . . . We are told that . . . Eratosthenes disapproved . . . of those who advised Alexander to treat Greeks as friends and barbarians as enemies: it would be more reasonable, he says, to make a division according to virtue and vice; . . . this was why Alexander disregarded all such advice and . . . conferred benefits upon all men of good repute. . . . So far there is no hint of Opis. But Tarn next brings in a passage in Plutarch's . . . "Fortune of Alexander"; there . . . Alexander is indeed credited with a cosmopolitan philosophy—as indeed it is the purpose of the [essay] to show that Alexander was a true philosopher. Plutarch first says that Zeno is much admired for the cosmopolitanism of his *Republic*, but that his ideal was translated into fact by Alexander. . . . Now, if Tarn had ascribed merely the general train of thought in the Plutarch passage . . . to Eratosthenes, we might well concede it. But that is just what he does not do: having "got the limits of the Eratosthenes fragment," he uses precisely the last part—the part where the differences between Strabo's citation and Plutarch are manifold and striking—with its divine mission and its loving-cup as being genuine Eratosthenes, saddling the philosopher with the ascription of these ideas to Alexander and even with the use of these actual words. It is then only a small step to the assertion that Eratosthenes' loving-cup did actually exist; it was the great krater on Alexander's table at Opis. It follows that Eratosthenes had before him an impressive eyewitness account of the banquet, which gave him the ideas he ascribes to Alexander—a much more impressive one than Ptolemy's account. . . . It should now be clear that none of this is solidly based. . . . We must firmly assign to the realm of fantasy any attempt to connect Eratosthenes with the enunciation of Alexander's divine mission [or] with the simile of the cup. . . . As for the Opis banquet, there is not a shred of evidence that Eratosthenes had ever heard of it. . . , and certainly none that he thought it more important than Ptolemy did.

4

CAESAR AND THE TIDE OF FORTUNE

In the two centuries preceding the beginning of the Christian era Rome conquered the Mediterranean world, dragging Hellenistic kings and sullen Western barbarians behind the chariots of the victors. Unfortunately, Rome was still a city-state and the ruling class viewed the empire primarily as a source of tribute and a field for military exploits. Roman citizenship had only been granted to the Italians after they rose in arms at the beginning of the first century B.C. The republic was indifferent to the rights of provincials, and justice was only obtained for them under the emperors. The powerful nobles who ran the republic had also let Rome become a vast slum, crowded with unemployed and wretched citizens who sold their votes for a pittance. In theory the republic was a democracy, in practice it was an oligarchy, but it was a failure as either. To vote, Romans had to come to the capital, which was impractical for most Italians and provincials. Power lay with the urban masses who filled the Tribal Assembly, which was the legislative body of Rome. The nobles in the Senate manipulated voters, handed out military commands and patronage, and ran the empire. As Mommsen has suggested, a representative voting system would have pumped new life from the provinces into the moribund republic, but the nobles and the masses at Rome were unwilling to surrender their monopoly on political power. In the first century B.C. the assembly was a constant scene of violence and bribery as bitter factions struggled to intimidate or win over voters.

The chief factions were the conservative Optimates and the more liberal Populares, but both groups were led by noble families whose rivalries wrecked the republic. Ideology meant little to the practical Romans who relished honors, power, and the opportunity to ruin an enemy. Two useful magistracies were the consulship and the tribunate—the two consuls were the executives of the Roman state, and each of the ten tribunes could veto any governmental action in the capital. In office, the consuls commanded armies and held military commands as proconsuls in the provinces after their term as consul had expired. Since all offices were annual, electioneering was constant and there was no relief from political pressures.

The armies, which were necessary for the safety and expansion of the Roman republic, became the instruments of its downfall. The generals were politicians who counted on the loyalty of their veterans as voters and in extreme cases used combat troops to overthrow a rival when political maneuvers failed. Early in the first century B.C. the conservative general Sulla stormed Rome, slaughtered his enemies, and established a brief dictatorship. While Pompey and Crassus were Sulla's henchmen, young Caesar belonged to the Populares. Sulla resigned after strengthening the oligarchic hold on the republic, but within a decade Pompey and Crassus joined forces with the Populares to win power; their trump cards were the armies. In 60 B.C. harassment by the Optimates drove Pompey, Crassus, and Caesar into a coalition, the First Triumvirate, which ran Rome and gave Caesar a chance to win glory in Gaul. By 50 B.C. Crassus had died in a war with Parthia, and Pompey and Caesar had fallen out. Since Gaul was subdued, Caesar's enemies tried to relieve him of his military command—they were confident of breaking Caesar because they had won the support of Pompey. The result was a terrible civil war which ended in the victory of Caesar, who assumed a lifetime dictatorship. The rule of one man made a mockery of the republic, but earlier three men and then two had made the major decisions at Rome. Thinking in terms of partnership, Caesar had been particularly distressed that his peer Pompey did not effect a compromise with him within the facade of constitutional forms. The dictatorship was not Caesar's aim—(he had wanted to run for consul in 49 B.C.)—but a poor expedient, forced upon him by circumstances.

So much of history is full of presumptuous dullards and homicidal maniacs that we are pleased to run across an intelligent and urbane man like Caesar. He was a prisoner of his time as all men are, but the dictator proved to be an exception to the rule of witless or vicious men who shape much of history. As a man, Caesar was most interesting. Highly intelligent, he wrote well and he had a realistic grasp of the needs of the provinces and the poor at Rome. Caesar was willing to grant citizenship to provincials and even placed some in the Senate; he also cut the relief rolls at Rome and resettled over a hundred thousand of the urban poor as property owners in the provinces. Too witty for his own good, Caesar was sarcastic and mocked his rivals—even worse, he was calculatingly merciful and spared their lives after defeating them. They never forgave the contempt which his clemency implied. Unlike Alexander, Caesar avoided alcohol and chased women. His celebrated affair with Cleopatra was a relaxation, not an infatuation with the ambitious young queen. Though he was merciful to Romans, Caesar was ruthless in Gaul, where on one occasion he had captured rebels mutilated; he also slaughtered the women and children of an invading German tribe. All in all, he was no self-styled messiah and certainly no humanitarian superman, but rather a very able Roman noble with many of the biases of his class. Sir Frank Adcock has said of Caesar: "His genius was the hard practical genius of Rome raised to the highest power: he was a keen edge on the old blade." To later generations, Caesar was a god and the ancestor of a dynasty; to some, he was the prototype of a power-mad tyrant. The latter image has no relevance to the Caesar of history.

The dictatorship of Caesar distressed some of his contemporaries, and it touches raw nerves today. Yet, words taken out of their historical context obscure realities, and the Roman republic was not a Platonic ideal but a very human institution. Sir Ronald Syme has some helpful comments on the use of words in politics and war:

The political cant of a country is naturally and always most strongly in evidence on the side of vested interests. In times of peace and prosperity it commands a wide measure of acquiescence, even of belief. Revolution rends the veil. But the revolution did not impede or annul the use of political fraud at Rome. On the contrary, the vocabulary was furbished up and adapted to a more modern and deadly technique. As commonly in civil strife and class-war, the relation between words and facts was inverted. Party-denominations prevailed entirely, and in the end success or failure became the only criterion of wisdom and of patriotism. In the service of faction, the fairest of pleas and the noblest of principles were assiduously enlisted. The art was as old as politics, its exponents required no mentors. The purpose of propaganda was threefold — to win an appearance of legality for measures of violence, to seduce the supporters of a rival party, and to stampede the neutral or non-political elements. First in value come freedom and orderly government, without the profession of which ideals no party can feel secure and sanguine, whatever be the acts of deception or violence in prospect. At Rome all men paid homage to liberty, holding it to be something roughly equivalent to the spirit and practice of republican government. Exactly what corresponded to the republican constitution was, however, a matter not of legal definition but of partisan interpretation. . . . The liberty of the Roman aristocrat meant the rule of a class and the perpetuation of privilege.[1]

Caesar must be judged as a Roman and a ruler, and not as the embodiment of dictatorship which may be distasteful to us. In Caesar we find none of the pompous egomania of Napoleon, the manic vulgarity of Hitler, or the icy cruelty of Stalin. Caesar had his Roman faults and neglected the political and social regeneration of Rome and the empire for an invasion of Parthia ostensibly to avenge Crassus. In the midst of his war plans, the dictator was murdered by his friends. Of the twenty-three wounds which pierced his body, only one in the chest was fatal — except for a chance blow, Caesar would have survived the attack on his life. How merciful would he then have been, or would Caesar have become another Sulla? His assassins claimed that he had wished to be a monarch, but Caesar had seen the shabby kings of the East and did not crave a crown — "I am no king," he grinned, "but Caesar!" Shakespeare, who relied on Plutarch's inept sermons, is a poor guide to history, but he caught the real reason for Caesar's murder in the speech which he put in Cassius' mouth:

[1] Sir Ronald Syme, *The Roman Revolution* (Oxford: Clarendon Press, 1939), pp. 154–155. Reprinted by permission.

Why, man, he doth bestride the narrow world
Like a Colossus, and we petty men
Walk under his huge legs and peep about
To find ourselves dishonorable graves.
Men at some time are masters of their fates.
The fault, dear Brutus, is not in our stars,
But in ourselves, that we are underlings.

Jealousy, not ideology, cut Caesar down.

The march of history is a chaotic thing, and we impose order on it at the risk of distorting the past. Men rarely know the ultimate results of their acts, and historians often impute motives which would surprise the actors, who like blind men stumble through a crisis to glory or defeat. To know the moment and direction for action is difficult, and luck is a decisive factor in history. Shakespeare realized this numbing imperative:

There is a tide in the affairs of men
Which, taken at the flood, leads on to fortune;
Omitted, all the voyage of their life
Is bound in shallows and in miseries.

In the mouth of Brutus, such words have particular irony and stunning truth. The future is dark, and behind any turn may lurk some horror undreamed of in our careful calculations. When he crossed the Rubicon, could Caesar have foreseen the Ides of March, Antony's war against the assassins, the long strife between Antony and Augustus, or the grim annals of the Julian dynasty? The future dictator was then caught in events not of his own making and he aptly used a gambler's phrase: "The die is cast."

VELLEIUS PATERCULUS

CAESAR: A ROMAN VIEW

Under Augustus and his successors, Caesar was treated with ambivalence by historians who reflected the government's view. Caesar the god had adopted the emperor Augustus, but Caesar the rebel set an embarrassing precedent for ambitious generals. Velleius Paterculus was an amateur historian and retired officer who had served loyally under Augustus and his successor Tiberius. His admiration of Tiberius was excessive but provides a useful antidote to the malice of Tacitus. Most Augustan writers maligned Mark Antony, and Paterculus was no exception. In the following passages, he damns Curio, who was Antony's friend. As Caesar's henchman, the tribune Curio proposed that both Caesar and Pompey disband their armies; by an overwhelming vote (370 to 22), the Senate approved Curio's proposal and thus demonstrated that the civil war was actually the result of a factious minority which was irreconcilably opposed to Caesar. The enemies of Caesar vetoed Curio's compromise. Despite the slur on Curio, Paterculus tried to be fair in describing the origins of the civil war and the behavior of Caesar in victory.

It was in Caesar's consulship [actually the year before in 60 B.C.] that there was formed between himself, Gnaeus Pompeius, and Marcus Crassus the partnership in political power which proved so baleful to the city, to the world, and subsequently at different periods to each of the triumvirs themselves. Pompey's motive in the adoption of this policy had been to secure through Caesar as consul the long delayed ratification of his acts in the provinces across the seas, to which . . . many still raised objections; Caesar agreed to it because he realized that in making this concession to the prestige of Pompey he would increase his own, and that by throwing on Pompey the odium for their joint control he would add to his own power; while Crassus hoped that by the influence of Pompey and the power of Caesar he might achieve a place of preeminence in the state which he had not been able to reach single-handed. Furthermore, a tie of marriage was cemented between Caesar and Pompey, in that Pompey now wedded Julia, Caesar's daughter. . . .

[Both Pompey and Crassus were jealous of Caesar's conquest of Gaul, and Crassus died in 53 B.C. in an abortive invasion of Parthia, where he had hoped to win similar glory.] About the fourth year of Caesar's stay in Gaul occurred the death of Julia [54 B.C.], the wife of Pompey, the one tie which bound together Pompey and Caesar in a coalition which, because of each one's jealousy of the other's power, held together with difficulty even during her lifetime; and as though fortune were bent upon breaking all the bonds between the two men destined for so great a conflict, Pompey's little son by Julia also died a short time afterwards. Then, inasmuch as agitation over the elections found vent in armed conflicts and civil bloodshed, which continued indefinitely and without check, Pompey was made consul for the third time [52 B.C.], now without a colleague, with the assent even of those who up to that time had opposed him for that office. The tribute paid him by this honor, which seemed to indicate his reconciliation with the Optimates, served

more than anything else to alienate him from Caesar. Pompey, however, employed his whole power during this consulship in curbing election abuses. . . .

It was not long after this that the first sparks of civil war were kindled. All fair-minded men desired that both Caesar and Pompey should disband their armies. Now Pompey in . . . [55 B.C.] had caused the provinces of Spain to be assigned to him, and though he was actually absent from them, administering the affairs of the city, he continued to govern them for three years through his lieutenants, . . . and while he agreed with those who insisted that Caesar should dismiss his army, he was opposed to those who urged that he should also dismiss his own. Had Pompey only died two years before the outbreak of hostilities, after the completion of his theater and the other public buildings with which he had surrounded it, at the time when he was attacked by a serious illness . . . and all Italy prayed for his safety as her foremost citizen, fortune would have lost the opportunity of overthrowing him and he would have borne to the grave unimpaired all the qualities of greatness that had been his in life. It was Gaius Curio, however, a tribune of the people, who, more than anyone else, applied the flaming torch which kindled the civil war and all the evils which followed for twenty consecutive years. Curio was a man of noble birth, eloquent, reckless, prodigal alike of his own fortune and chastity and of those of other people, a man of the utmost cleverness in perversity, who used his gifted tongue for the subversion of the state. No wealth and no pleasures sufficed to satiate his appetites. He was at first on the side of Pompey, that is to say, as it was then regarded, on the side of the republic. Then he pretended to be opposed both to Pompey and Caesar, but in his heart he was for Caesar. Whether his conversion was spontaneous or due to a bribe of ten million sesterces [$500,000.00?], as is reported, we shall leave undetermined. Finally, when a truce was on the point of being concluded on terms of the most salutary character, terms

From Velleius Paterculus, II 44, 47–49, 56–58. Reprinted by permission of the publishers and the Loeb Classical Library from Frederick W. Shipley, trans., *Velleius Paterculus* (Cambridge, Mass.: Harvard University Press, 1955; London: William Heinemann Ltd.), pp. 145–47, 153–61, 173–77.

which were demanded in a spirit of the utmost fairness by Caesar and accepted by Pompey without protest, it was in the end broken and shattered by Curio in spite of Cicero's extraordinary efforts to preserve harmony in the state. . . . [Paterculus apparently refers to a proposal for a new reassignment of provinces, which was vetoed by Curio because it would leave Caesar without an army until he could be elected consul again. Caesar was authorized to run for the office while absent from Rome.]

In the consulship of Lentulus and Marcellus . . . [49 B.C.] the civil war burst into flame. The one leader seemed to have the better cause, the other the stronger; on the one was the appearance, on the other the reality of power; Pompey was armed with the authority of the Senate, Caesar with the devotion of his soldiers. The consuls and the Senate conferred the supreme authority not on Pompey but on his cause. No effort was omitted by Caesar that could be tried in the interest of peace, but no offer of his was accepted by the Pompeians. Of the two consuls, one showed more bitterness than was fair, the other, Lentulus, could not save himself from ruin without bringing ruin upon the state, while Marcus Cato insisted that they should fight to the death rather than allow the republic to accept a single dictate from a mere citizen. The stern Roman of the old-fashioned type would praise the cause of Pompey, the politic would follow the lead of Caesar, recognizing that while there was on the one side greater prestige, the other was the more formidable.

When at last, rejecting all the demands of Caesar who was content to retain the title to the province [of Cisalpine Gaul and Illyricum] with but a single legion, the Senate decreed that he should enter the city as a private citizen and should as such submit himself to the votes of the Roman people in his candidacy for the consulship, Caesar concluded that war was inevitable and crossed the Rubicon with his army. Gnaeus Pompeius, the consuls, and the majority of the Senate abandoned first the city, then Italy, and crossed the sea to [Greece]. . . . [In 48 B.C. Caesar defeated Pompey at Pharsalus and later occupied Cleopatra's Egypt where the fugitive Pompey had been murdered. In 46 B.C. Caesar defeated his enemies in Africa at the battle of Thapsus. Rather than accept Caesar's clemency, Cato killed himself. In 45 B.C. Caesar defeated the last of the Pompeians at Munda in Spain, and the civil war was over.]

Caesar, victorious over all his enemies, returned to the city and pardoned all who had borne arms against him, an act of generosity almost passing belief. . . . But it was the lot of this great man, who behaved with such clemency in all his victories, that his peaceful enjoyment of supreme power should last but five months. For, returning to the city in October, he was slain on the Ides of March [44 B.C.]. Brutus and Cassius were the leaders of the conspiracy. He had failed to win the former by the promise of the consulship and had offended the latter by the postponement of his candidacy. There were also in the plot to compass his death some of the most intimate of all his friends, who owed their elevation to the success of his party, namely Decimus Brutus, Gaius Trebonius, and others of illustrious name. Marcus Antonius, his colleague in the consulship, ever ready for acts of daring, had brought great odium upon Caesar by placing a royal crown upon his head as he sat on the rostra at the Lupercalia. Caesar put the crown from him, but in such a way that he did not seem to be displeased.

In the light of experience, due credit should be given to the counsel of Pansa and Hirtius, who had always warned Caesar that he must hold by arms the position which he had won by arms. But Caesar kept reiterating that he would rather die than live in fear, and while he looked for a return for the clemency he had shown, he was taken off his guard by men devoid of gratitude, although the gods gave many signs and presages of the threatened danger. For the soothsayers had warned him beforehand carefully to beware the Ides of March; his wife Calpurnia, terrified by a dream, kept begging him to remain at home on that day; and notes warning him of the conspiracy were handed him, but he neglected to read them at the time. But verily the power of destiny is inevitable; it confounds the judgment of him whose fortune it has determined to reverse. . . . Cassius had been in favor of slaying Antony as well as Caesar and of destroying Caesar's will, but Brutus had opposed him, insisting that citizens ought not to seek the blood of any but the "tyrant" — for to call Caesar "tyrant" placed his deed in a better light.

JULIUS CAESAR

"THEY WOULD HAVE IT SO"

A man's testimony on his own controversial actions is never impartial, often dangerous, and always useful, for it reveals the mind of the man if not the truth of the matter. In 48 B.C. Caesar justified his position by writing an account of the outbreak of the civil war which was still raging. Concerning Book I of Caesar's *Civil War,* Sir Frank Adcock has written: "Caesar is an advocate for himself, not wholly scrupulous, but wholly sincere. It is plain that he believed that he had not received the treatment which his exploits and his dignity deserved, and that his army shared his belief. He did not seek to overthrow the Republican constitution, but only to have it work for his interests and not against them. He was prepared to meet his enemies at least part of the way provided he did not forfeit his career, to come to terms with Pompey in a new coalition in which, however, he would be at an advantage over his former ally. The civic dissension need not be a civil war; it was not by his choosing that his enemies made it one. As he said at Pharsalus, 'they would have it so.'"[1] Caesar, of course, was not present at the Senate meetings which he described, but he had reliable information from the Senate's stenographers and from his supporters who did attend the debates. Late in 50 B.C., Caesar sent a letter to the Senate offering to resign his military command if Pompey would also give up his troops.

My letter was delivered to the consuls, but it was a difficult matter to get permission for it to be read aloud in front of the Senate. Indeed permission was only granted after the most vigorous agitation on the part of the people's tribunes. As for having a regular debate on the contents of the letter, it was found impossible to secure this concession at all. Instead, the consuls proceeded to bring in a motion on the political situation in general. The consul Lucius Lentulus addressed the Senate in a provocative manner. He assured them that he would play his full part in the defense of the republic, if the senators themselves would only show daring and resolution in the expression of their opinions. "If, on the other hand," he said, "as has happened on previous occasions, you are going to let your thoughts turn toward Caesar and the prospects of making yourselves popular in that direction, then I, Lentulus, am going to make my own decisions without reference to you. I too can, if I like, make myself safe by accepting Caesar's favor and Caesar's friendship." Scipio then made a speech to the same effect. Pompey, he said, was prepared to play his part in the defense of the republic, so long as the Senate would follow his lead; if, however, the Senate showed weakness and hesitation now, though they might beg for his help in the future they would beg for it in vain.

As the meeting of the Senate was being held in Rome and as Pompey was near the city at the time, it was considered that this speech of Scipio's had been dictated to him by Pompey himself. There were a few senators who expressed more moderate views. . . . There was Marcus Calidius who proposed that, in order that there should be no reason for a recourse to arms, Pompey should leave Italy and go to his provinces. "Caesar," he said, "has had two legions taken away from him by Pompey and is

[1] Sir Frank E. Adcock, *Caesar as Man of Letters* (Cambridge: Cambridge University Press, 1956), pp. 46–47.

From *War Commentaries of Caesar,* translated by Rex Warner, pp. 211–14, 217–18, ©1960 by Rex Warner. Published by arrangement with The New American Library, Inc., New York.

now apprehensive because of the impression that Pompey is holding these legions in reserve and keeping them near Rome with the idea of using them against him." Marcus Rufus also made a speech very much in the same terms as that of Calidius. All these speakers were vigorously attacked by the consul Lucius Lentulus in the most violent language. Lentulus absolutely refused to allow any discussion of the proposal of Calidius. . . . So, as a result of the consul's angry words, of the terror caused by an army actually on the spot, and of the threats of Pompey's friends, the Senate adopted the proposal of Scipio, the majority of the senators voting under force and pressure and against their wills. Scipio's proposal was that Caesar should disband his army before a fixed date, and that, if he failed to do so, he should be considered a public enemy. At this point, the people's tribunes, Mark Antony and Quintus Cassius, interposed their veto. Immediately the Senate was required to discuss whether this veto should be regarded as valid or not—a weighty and serious discussion—and the more bitter and savage a speech was, the more it was cheered by my enemies. The meeting of the Senate ended in the evening and all senators were then invited to visit Pompey outside the city. Pompey offered his congratulations to those who had shown themselves ready for action and encouraged them to preserve the same spirit in the future; he spoke sharply to the more lukewarm members and urged them to change their attitude. . . . Pressure was brought to bear on all who were friends of the consuls and all who were supporters of Pompey or of my old enemies to attend meetings of the Senate, and so vocal a crowd had the effect of terrifying the weaker spirits and forcing their own views on those whose minds were not made up. . . .

Other proposals . . . were made for sending a deputation to me to explain what the feelings of the Senate were. Every one of these speakers and every one of the proposals were attacked and opposed in speeches made by the consul, by Scipio, and by Cato. Cato was activated by his long hatred of me and by his bitter feelings at having failed in the elections [for consul in 51 B.C.]. The behavior of Lentulus can be explained by the fact that he had enormous debts and was looking forward to the command of an army and of provinces and to the bribes he would acquire for bestowing regal titles on native rulers; he boasted among his friends that he was going to become another Sulla, with supreme power in his hands. Scipio too was motivated by the

expectation of a province and of armies which, since he was Pompey's father-in-law, he thought he ought to share with him; other motives can be found in the fact that he was frightened of prosecution, that he had a violent, ostentatious character himself and was led on by the flattery of men of like character who at this time had great influence both in politics and in the law courts. As to Pompey, he had been pushed into action by my enemies and also by his own wish that no one should be placed on the same level as himself. He had entirely broken off his old friendship with me and had become friends again with those who had been enemies of us both, most of whom he personally had turned against me during the time that he was my son-in-law. He was also concerned about the discredit he had brought on himself by keeping back the two legions to serve his power and supremacy instead of allowing them to go to Asia and Syria. Therefore, Pompey was eager to have things settled by force of arms. . . .

[On January 7, 49 B.C., the Senate decreed a state of emergency.] Decrees of the most savage and of the most insulting kind were passed depriving me of my command and the tribunes of their rights and dignity. The tribunes immediately fled from Rome and joined me at Ravenna where I was waiting to receive a reply to my own very moderate demands and hoping that a certain sense of fairness might be shown so that everything could end peacefully. . . . [On January 11, Caesar led the Thirteenth Legion across the Rubicon river which was the border of his province; the civil war had begun. Still hoping for a compromise settlement with his rival, Caesar sent a personal message to Pompey:] "I have always . . . put the good name and honor of the state first and have regarded them as more valuable than life itself. What distressed me was to find that my enemies in the most insulting manner were taking from me a privilege that had been granted to me by the Roman people. I was being deprived of six months of my command and was being dragged back to Rome, although the people had ratified the proposal that I should be allowed to stand for the consulship at the next elections without being personally present. Nevertheless, for the sake of the state I accepted this infringement of my rights and attack upon my honor with a good grace. But when I sent a letter to the Senate proposing that both sides should disband their armies, I failed even to gain this point. Troops are being raised all over Italy; two legions, stolen from me on the pretext that they were to be used against Parthia, are still in the country;

the whole state is under arms. How can all this be explained except on the assumption that there is a plan to destroy me? Yet for the sake of the state I am still prepared to make any concession and to put up with anything. I propose that Pompey should go to his provinces, that both of us should disband our armies, that everyone in Italy should return to civilian life, that the state should be freed from fear, that the holding of free elections and the general control of affairs should be handed over to the Senate and the Roman people. In order that this should be done with as little trouble as possible and on fixed terms which should be ratified by oath, I propose that either Pompey should come nearer to me or else should allow me to come nearer to him. A conference between the two of us would have the effect of settling all difficulties." . . .

[The consuls and Pompey insisted that Caesar retire to Gaul and disband his troops before Pompey would go to Spain; until Caesar promised to do so, they would continue to prepare for war.] These terms were unfair. It was unfair of Pompey to demand that I should retire to Gaul while he kept both his provinces and the legions that did not belong to him; to want me to disband my troops while he himself continued to recruit new forces; to promise to go to his province, but give no definite date for when he would do so. Thus, even if he stayed in Italy until my consulship was over, he could not be considered guilty of having broken his word. Finally, what showed that there was very little real hope of peace was the fact that Pompey allowed no time for a conference and made no suggestion that he should come near me personally.

THEODOR MOMMSEN

"CAESAR: THE PERFECT MAN"

Theodor Mommsen (1817–1903) of the University of Berlin was one of the giants of modern scholarship. Through his numerous essays and a monumental collection of Latin inscriptions, he helped to convert the study of ancient history into a critical discipline. Mommsen was a literary artist as well as a scientific historian, and he was awarded the first Nobel prize for literature in 1902. He wrote his immensely popular and influential *History of Rome* (1854–1856) when he was a young professor anxious for fame and money. In politics, Mommsen was a liberal and served in the German Reichstag, where he battled Bismarck on a number of occasions. As a professor, he opposed outbursts of anti-Semitism and ultranationalism on German campuses and staunchly defended academic freedom against religious bigots. His hatred of Prussian Junkers was so great that it warped his understanding of the late Roman republic. Despite his great learning, Mommsen saw the conservative opponents of Caesar as muddle-headed reactionaries and decadent caricatures of his hated Junkers. The partisan historian labeled Cato as a "stupid Don Quixote" and dismissed Pompey as a glorified sergeant major. His extreme adulation of Caesar as the "perfect man" was unscholarly, but Mommsen felt deeply about politics and Caesar seemed to him to have been a superhuman scourge of Junkers. Because of Mommsen's great prestige, his romantic image of Caesar has impressed uncritical readers as the verdict of history.

When Caesar was informed by the tribunes who had fled to his camp of the reception which his propos-

als had met in the capital, he called together the soldiers of the thirteenth legion . . . and unfolded before them the state of things. It was not merely the man of genius versed in the knowledge of men's hearts, whose brilliant eloquence shone forth in this gripping crisis of his own and the world's destiny. It was not even the generous and victorious commander-in-chief addressing soldiers whom he himself had called to arms, and who for eight years had followed his banners with daily increasing enthusiasm. There spoke, above all, the energetic and consistent statesman, who had now for nine-and-twenty years defended the cause of freedom in good times and bad; who had braved for it the daggers of assassins and the executioners of the aristocracy, the swords of the Germans and the waves of the unknown ocean, without ever yielding or wavering; who had torn to pieces the Sullan constitution, overthrown the rule of the Senate, and furnished the defenseless and unarmed democracy with protection and arms by means of the struggle beyond the Alps. And he spoke not to the Roman public, whose republican enthusiasm had been long burnt down to ashes and dross, but to the young men from the towns and villages of Northern Italy, who still felt freshly and purely the mighty influence of the thought of civic freedom; who were still capable of fighting and dying for ideals; who had themselves received for their country in a revolutionary way from Caesar the citizenship which the Roman government had refused. . . . And when he, the leader and general of the popular party, summoned the soldiers of the people, now that conciliatory means had been exhausted and concession had reached its utmost limits, to follow him in the last, the inevitable, the decisive struggle against the equally hated and despised, equally perfidious and incapable, and in fact ludicrously incorrigible aristocracy, not an officer or a soldier could hold back. . . .

Few men have had their elasticity so thoroughly tested as Caesar, sole creative genius of Rome and the last produced by the ancient world, which accordingly followed the path he marked for it until its sun was set. . . . Caesar was thoroughly a realist and a man of sense; and whatever he undertook was pervaded and guided by the cool sobriety which is the most characteristic mark of his genius. . . . To this he owed the "marvelous serenity" which remained steadily with him through good and evil days; to this he owed his complete independence, uninfluenced by favorite, by mistress, or even by

friend. As a result of this clarity of judgment Caesar never formed illusions regarding the power of fate and the ability of man. . . . As occasionally the most sagacious men enter into a pure game of hazard, so Caesar's rationalism at some points made contact with mysticism. Such gifts could not fail to produce a statesman. From early youth, accordingly, Caesar was a statesman in the truest sense, with the highest aim which a man is allowed to set for himself—the political, military, intellectual, and moral regeneration of his own deeply decayed nation, and of the still more deeply decayed Hellenic nation joined to his own. The hard school of thirty years' experience changed his views as to how this aim might be reached, but his aim itself remained constant both in time of hopeless humiliation and of unlimited power, both when as demagogue and conspirator he stole toward it by paths of darkness, and when as joint ruler and then as sole monarch he worked at his task before the eyes of the world. . . . A born ruler, he governed the minds of men as the wind drives the clouds. . . .

Caesar was monarch, but he was never seized with the giddiness of the tyrant. He is perhaps the only one among the earth's great who in large matters and small never acted from impulse or caprice, but always according to his duty as ruler, and who might look back on his life and doubtless find erroneous calculations to deplore, but no false step of passion to regret. . . . Such was this unique man, so easy and yet so infinitely difficult to describe. His whole nature is transparent clarity. . . . The secret lies in its perfection. As a man no less than as a historical figure, Caesar occupies a position where the great contrasts of existence meet and balance. . . .

Caesar was the entire and perfect man . . . just because more than any other he placed himself amid the currents of his time, and because more than any other he epitomized the essential peculiarity of the Roman nation—practical aptitude as a citizen. . . . As the artist can paint everything save consummate beauty, so the historian, when once in a thousand years he encounters perfection, can only be silent. For normality is doubtless capable of being described, but only by the negative notion of the absence of defect. Nature's secret, whereby she combines normality and individuality in her most finished productions, is beyond expression. We can

From Theodor Mommsen, *The History of Rome*, ed. Dero A. Saunders and John H. Collins (Cleveland and New York, 1958), pp. 386–88, 479, 481–82, 484–87, 496–97, 595–96. Copyright © 1958 by the World Publishing Company. All rights reserved. Reprinted by permission.

"Caesar: The Perfect Man"

only deem fortunate those who beheld this perfection, and gain some faint conception of it from the reflected luster which rests imperishably on the creations of so great a nature. . . .

It is proper to . . . protest against the custom—common alike to simplicity and perfidy—of using historical praise and censure as phrases of general application with no regard for circumstances. The present case involves construing the judgment of Caesar into a judgment of what is called Caesarism. . . . In this sense the history of Caesar and of Roman Imperialism, with all the unsurpassed greatness of the master worker, with all the historical necessity of the work, is in truth a sharper censure of modern autocracy than could be written by the hand of man. According to the same natural law by which the smallest organism infinitely surpasses the most artistic machine, every constitution, however defective, which expresses the free will of the majority infinitely surpasses the most brilliant and humane absolutism; for the former is capable of growth and therefore living, while the latter is what it is and therefore dead.

This law of nature demonstrates itself all the more completely in the Roman military monarchy, in that under the impulse of its creator's genius and in the absence of all foreign pressures, that monarchy developed in purer form than in any similar state. From Caesar's time . . . the Roman system had only an external coherence, repeating itself only mechanically; while internally, even under Caesar it was utterly withered and dead. If in its early stages and above all in Caesar's own soul, the hopeful dream of combining free popular development and absolute rule was still cherished, the government of the highly gifted emperors of the Julian house soon taught men a terrible lesson in how far it was possible to hold fire and water in the same vessel.

Caesar's work was salutary and necessary not because it was or could be a blessing in itself. But given the social organization of antiquity based on slavery and utterly foreign to republican-constitutional representation, and under the organization of the urban constitution which during five hundred years had ripened into oligarchic absolutism, an absolute military monarchy was both a logical necessity and the least of evils. When the slave-holding aristocracy of Virginia and the Carolinas shall have carried matters as far as their predecessors in Sullan Rome, Caesarism will there too be legitimized at the bar of history; where it appears under other circumstances, it is at once a caricature and a usurpation. But history will not deny the true Caesar his due honor, because her verdict in the presence of bad Caesars may lead fools astray and give rogues occasion for lying and fraud. . . . [In the second edition, Mommsen added a note to this passage:] When this was written—in the year 1857—no one could foresee how soon the mightiest struggle and the most glorious victory as yet recorded in human annals would save the United States from this fearful trial and secure the future existence of an absolute self-governing freedom not to be permanently kept in check by any local Caesarism. . . .

Caesar, wherever he acted as a destroyer, only carried out the pronounced verdict of historical development. . . . With the same self-reliant genius that accomplished the regeneration of Rome, he undertook also the regeneration of the Hellenes and resumed the interrupted work of the great Alexander whose image, we may well believe, was never absent from Caesar's soul. . . . [He] created, out of a state without distinctive culture or cosmopolitan civilization, a new whole in which culture and state again met in the rich fullness of blessed maturity. These are the outlines which Caesar drew for this work, according to which he himself labored, and according to which posterity—for many centuries confined to the paths which this great man marked out—endeavored to work generally in accordance with the intentions of the illustrious master, if not with his intellect and energy. Little was finished, much was merely begun. Whether the plan was complete, those who venture to vie in thought with such a man may decide. We observe no material defect in what lies before us. Every single stone of the building is enough to make a man immortal, yet all combine to form one harmonious whole.

JOHN H. COLLINS

CAESAR AND THE CORRUPTION OF POWER

Not all scholars have seen Caesar in a favorable light. Men of the twentieth century have witnessed too many sawdust Caesars and ersatz emperors to be able to read Mommsen without skepticism. John H. Collins of Northern Illinois University is a distinguished classicist who recanted on Mommsen's Caesar. His essay on "Caesar and the Corruption of Power" is lively and personally revealing. Whether or not he is correct in his indictment of Caesar, Collins has overstated the role of Cleopatra who, after all, was not "the serpent of the Nile." Before she was born, Caesar had seen Eastern luxury and vice in Bithynia, and when he dallied with Cleopatra, the dictator was a middle-aged man of the world and not an impressionable youth. As for Caesar's high-handed behavior as master of Rome, the details come from questionable sources and ultimately stem from the propaganda of his assassins. Caesar as Lucifer is no more plausible than Caesar as Messiah.

The figure of Caesar offered us in Shakespeare's play does not easily harmonize with the Caesar of the Commentaries, that is to say, with the Caesar of "history." Shakespeare's Caesar is a vain, pompous, cantankerous, aging egoist. . . . Of the farseeing statesman, the military genius, the master leader of men, . . . Shakespeare gives scarcely a hint in the earlier acts of the play . . . It is only after the murder that Caesar assumes this shape of greatness.

Thou art the ruins of the noblest man
That ever lived in the tide of times.
The foremost man of all this world.

I well recall the vague questioning that filled my beginner's mind when, fresh from the strong impression of Shakespeare, "at the cost of many tears and some blood I purchased the knowledge of Latin syntax" through the medium of the *Gallic War*. It seemed there were two Caesars, a great and a small, a leader and a tyrant. Some years later I read for the first time the brilliant chapter of Mommsen and under his powerful influence, became an incurable Caesarian. . . .

Although the great Caesar, Mommsen's Caesar, is . . . victorious on all major fronts, the human, all-too-human Caesar of Shakespeare cannot quite be relegated to the unhistorical region of subjective imagination. Aside from the fact that Shakespeare commanded a knowledge of human nature deeper than that of any other man of whom we have record, the purely historical evidence in favor of his general vision is weighty and derived from many independent sources. The honorific titles and privileges, the arrogant utterances and acts, the contemptuous disregard of the great traditions of the Roman republic that one finds catalogued in every biography of Caesar go far toward justifying the final condemnation of Suetonius [a biographer and gossipmonger of the second century A.D.] — "it was felt that Caesar had misused despotic power and was justly cut down." . . .

Out of the last eighteen months of Caesar's life, and more particularly out of the last six months, we have reports of a series of sayings and incidents, mostly from the secondary writers, but the most important also from Cicero, demonstrating a contempt for the republic and a striving for kingly and even divine honors in crass contradiction of the ancestral ways. . . . Suetonius, whose judgment must not be undervalued, devotes five chapters to Caesar's arrogance and insults. . . . The overall impression is that of a grovelling adulation by the Senate in the heaping up of titles and extravagant honors, and of

From John H. Collins, "Caesar and the Corruption of Power," *Historia*, IV (1955), pp. 445–46, 452–53, 455–58, 461–62, 464–65. Reprinted by permission of Franz Steiner Verlag, publishers of *Historia*.

an excessive power-lust on the part of Caesar. His conduct passed beyond occasional tactlessness or petulance; it shows deliberate and habitual insolence. The assumption of the life-time dictatorship in January 44, in flat contradiction of all Roman constitutional tradition, and the slightly later scene on the Lupercalia were merely the climax of a long course of usurpation. . . .

As is well known, the assassination of Caesar was called by Goethe "the most senseless deed in all history," and the verdict has been generally accepted by modern students. But leaving aside the question of its sense or folly, I would point out that it was also the result of the most successful plot in all history. Some sixty men were members of the conspiracy; it was discussed weeks if not months in advance . . . —yet the secret was not betrayed. History records many an assassination and many a plot, but the assassination of Caesar is absolutely unique in its elaboration and success. For a comparable murder plot we must look to the twentieth century and the attempt on Hitler in July 1944. The analogy is suggestive. The attack on Hitler was made by men who had grown desperate and who saw no means other than political murder of serving their country or of saving what might yet be saved. Knowing their circumstances, we do not judge them as criminals. Is it quite certain that we know enough about the Roman situation of 44 B.C. to be able to reverse the unanimous sentence of those sixty senators?

In calling attention to the case of Hitler, I have no wish to set up a general comparison or to see in Caesar an ancient fascist. I mean only to emphasize the extraordinary intensity of the hatred he had brought upon himself, and the amazing solidarity of his enemies. Few men can have reached such a degree of human isolation. Caesar's loneliness has been remarked by many of his biographers; it is less often remarked how far he had moved in his last months from the human geniality of the years in Gaul. . . . The tragedy of Caesar lies not so much in the fact that he was murdered by his friends, as in the fact that in the end he had no friends left, and had become such a menace to all that the best thought of the day identified with liberty and patriotism that sixty men could be found ready to risk their lives to kill him.

Modern opinion of Caesar has naturally been strongly colored by modern condemnation of the old republican system. The liberty for which Cicero so longed and for which Cato laid down his life meant in practice the liberty of a few hundred men to parasitize the Mediterranean world, and the liberty of . . . gangsters . . . to terrorize the capital. . . . But such considerations cannot be called on to justify Caesar's ruthless trampling on established and venerable forms unless it can be shown that he himself had some genuine vision of a future Reichsstaat in which the general welfare would replace the old game played for money and prestige. Such a vision has indeed been attributed to him, but its documentation is regrettably inadequate. . . . It is difficult to avoid the feeling that Caesar was thinking about out-Alexandering Alexander [as he prepared to invade Parthia]. It is possible that the Ides of March forestalled a military shipwreck comparable with Napoleon's disaster in Russia. The sure realism of Caesar's Gallic period had given way to dreams of world conquest. . . .

It appears to the present writer that we may profitably accept the ancient tradition with less of modern subtlety and modern re-interpretation than has usually been applied. It is not so much the ancient sources as our modern ways of thought that must be critically scrutinized to reach the historical truth. Our four best witnesses—Romans, drenched in Roman mores—Caesar himself, Cicero, Sallust, and Suetonius . . . , all tell essentially the same story. It is the story of a noble, genial, incomparably gifted nature corrupted by absolute power, quite in the sense of Lord Acton's famous aphorism. And the corruption of power, in Caesar's case, was aggravated by circumstances of enormous temptation, adequate to account for the fall of an archangel. . . .

Once the [civil] war had begun, Caesar continued to seek a compromise peace and demanded no extra-constitutional powers as the price. All his overtures were rejected, and the war went on to the bitter end. It would be impossible to imagine circumstances more conducive to hardening him into a cynical contempt for human stupidity. A second important factor in effecting the visible change in Caesar's character was, I cannot but think, the influence of Cleopatra and of the atmosphere of oriental pomp and luxury that Caesar found in Egypt. . . . The evidence that Cleopatra was still an important factor in Caesar's plans at the time of his death is supported by Cicero, and Augustus, at least, took the matter seriously enough to order the execution, on no visible grounds, of the young Caesarion.[1] . . . It does neither Caesar nor Cleopatra justice to degrade this vast human drama to the level of a scandal. With good right did the Romans a few years later fear Cleopatra "as they had feared none other but Hannibal." [Tarn's phrase.] I have suggested above that the Ides of March may have saved Rome from a military disaster in the Parthian desert. Quite as possibly they may have saved Rome and Europe for the West. . . .

There is adequate evidence that Caesar underwent a major change in character and outlook in his last phase, a change of character marked by cynicism and arrogance. It was a change which grew out of his disillusionment with his fellow citizens and with his older political ideals. It is less true to say that he rejected the republic than to say that the republic

[1] Cleopatra claimed that Caesarion was Caesar's son, and Antony recognized the claim. As the adopted son of Caesar, Augustus could not tolerate a rival; he also killed Antony's oldest son. [Editor's note.]

rejected him. His enormous genius shattered itself upon the impossible task of making the republic fit to rule the empire, and he turned to despotism in contempt and perhaps in bitterness. . . . An important factor in the outlook of his last years was undoubtedly the influence of Cleopatra. It would be too much to say that Caesar had become "orientalized" or "un-Roman," but that the flesh-pots of Egypt had touched him not at all is improbable in itself and against the weight of the evidence. A progressive megalomania shows itself in his conduct after Thapsus, and particularly after Munda. The insight of Blake.

The strongest poison ever known
Came from Caesar's laurel crown,

is justified by the history of his astounding career. The judgment of his contemporaries was more accurate than that of most modern reconstructions, and though the good that he did lived after him, it lived by wills and forces other than his.

SIR RONALD SYME

CAESAR: A MODERN VIEW

Sir Ronald Syme of the University of Oxford is the most respected living authority on the history of Rome. In influence, he must be ranked with Gibbon and Mommsen. Born in New Zealand, Syme brought a "colonial" irreverence for authority to the study of Roman history. Many British scholars had identified the Roman Empire with Britannia's world sway and transformed Augustus into a proper British gentleman. Mommsen believed that Augustus was sincerely concerned with republican ideals, and the great German had convinced most scholars that the factions of the late Roman republic were political parties in the nineteenth-century sense. However, Syme harkened to earlier masters and embraced the lapidary style and trenchant pessimism of Tacitus and Gibbon. His *Roman Revolution* (1939) was an epoch-making study of the collapse of the republic and the establishment of the new order of Augustus. Impatient with slogans and images, Syme views politics as a struggle of men for power and not a conflict of vague ideas: "Power and chance are the presiding divinities." In Britain and abroad, the influence of Syme has been great on the postwar generation of scholars and students.

In all ages, whatever the form and name of government, be it monarchy, republic, or democracy, an oligarchy lurks behind the facade; and Roman history, republican or imperial, is the history of the governing class. . . . During the civil wars every party and every leader professed to be defending the cause of liberty and of peace. Those ideals were incompatible. When peace came, it was the peace of despotism. . . . The political life of the Roman republic was stamped and swayed, not by parties and programmes of a modern and parliamentary character, not by the ostensible opposition between Senate and people, Optimates and Populares, nobles and new men, but by the strife for power, wealth, and glory. The contestants were the nobles among themselves, as individuals or in groups, open in the elections and in the courts of law, or masked by secret intrigue. . . . The Roman constitution was a screen and a sham. . . . The general had to be a politician, for his legionaries were a host of clients, looking to their leader for spoil in war and estates in Italy when their campaigns were over. But not veterans only were attached to his cause—from his provincial commands the dynast won to his allegiance and personal following . . . towns and whole regions, provinces and nations, kings and tetrarchs. Such were the resources which ambition required to win power in Rome and direct the policy of the imperial republic as consul or as one of the leaders. . . .

The leaders strove for prestige and power, but not to erect a despotic rule upon the ruins of the constitution or to carry out a real revolution. The constitution served the purposes of generals or of demagogues well enough. When Pompeius returned [in 62 B.C.] from the East, he lacked the desire as well as the pretext to march on Rome; and Caesar did not conquer Gaul in the design of invading Italy with a great army to establish a military autocracy. Their ambitions and their rivalries might have been tolerated in a small city-state or in a Rome that was merely the head of an Italian confederation. In the capital of the world they were anachronistic and ruinous. . . . The remedy was simple and drastic. For the health of the Roman people, the dynasts had to go. Augustus completed the purge and created the new state. . . .

In the autumn [of 50 B.C.] men began to speak of an inevitable war. Fortune was arranging the scene for a grand and terrible spectacle. Caesar would tolerate no superior, Pompeius no rival. Caesar had many enemies, provoked by his ruthless ambition, by his acts of arrogance towards other leaders—and by his support, when consul and proconsul, of the domination of Pompeius, who now, for supreme power, seemed likely to throw over his ally. On December 1st Curio's proposal [to disband both armies] came up in the Senate again, revealing an overpowering majority against both dynasts. . . . Then followed debate in the Senate, public attempts at mediation and negotiation in private. On January 1st a proposal of Caesar was rejected and he was declared contumacious: six days later his province was taken from him. The Caesarian tribunes M. Antonius and Q. Cassius, their veto disregarded, fled from the city. A state of emergency was proclaimed. Even had Pompeius now wished to avert the appeal to arms, he was swept forward by uncontrollable forces, entangled in the embrace of perfidious allies: or, as he called it himself, patriotic submission to the needs of the commonwealth. The coalition may summarily be described as four ancient and eminent families, linked closely with one another and with the Catonian faction. . . . It was the oligarchy of Sulla, manifest and menacing in its last bid for power, serried but insecure. Pompeius was playing a double game. He hoped to employ the leading nobles to destroy Caesar, whether it came to war or not, in either way gaining the mastery. They were not duped—they knew Pompeius: but they fancied that Pompeius, weakened by the loss of his ally and of popular support, would be in their power at last, amenable to guidance or to be discarded if recalcitrant. The policy arose from the brain and will of Marcus Cato. His allies, eager to enlist a man of principle on their side, celebrated as integrity what was often conceit or stupidity and mistook craft for sagacity. They might have known better—Cato's stubborn refusal to agree to the land bill for Pompeius' veterans [in 61 B.C.] only led to worse evils and a subverting of the constitution. After long strife against the domination of Pompeius, Cato resolved to support a dictatorship, though anxiously shunning the name. Cato's confidence in his own rectitude and insight derived secret strength from the antipathy which he felt for . . . Caesar. . . .

The conquest of Gaul, the war against Pompeius and the establishment of the dictatorship of Caesar are events that move in a harmony so swift and sure as to appear pre-ordained; and history has sometimes been written as though Caesar set the tune from the beginning, in the knowledge that monarchy was the panacea for the world's ills and with the design to achieve it by armed force. Such a view is too simple to be historical. . . . As the artful motion

From Sir Ronald Syme, *The Roman Revolution* (Oxford, 1939), pp. 7, 9, 11, 15, 38, 41–43, 45–51, 53, 59. Reprinted by permission of The Clarendon Press.

of a Caesarian tribune had revealed, an overwhelming majority in the Senate, nearly four hundred against twenty-two, wished both dynasts to lay down their extraordinary commands. A rash and factious minority prevailed. . . . Upon Caesar they had thrust the choice between civil war and political extinction. But Caesar refused to join the long roll of Pompeius' victims. . . . If he gave way now, it was the end. Returning to Rome as a private citizen, Caesar would at once be prosecuted by his enemies for extortion or treason. They would secure lawyers reputed for eloquence, high principle and patriotism. Cato was waiting for him, rancorous and incorruptible. A jury carefully selected, with moral support from soldiers of Pompeius stationed around the court, would bring in the inevitable verdict. After that, nothing remained for Caesar but to join the exiled Milo at Massilia and enjoy the red mullet and Hellenic culture of that university city.

Caesar was constrained to appeal to his army for protection. At last the enemies of Caesar had succeeded in ensnaring Pompeius and in working the constitution against the craftiest politician of the day: he was declared a public enemy if he did not lay down his command before a certain day. By invoking constitutional sanctions against Caesar, a small faction misrepresented the true wishes of a vast majority in the Senate, in Rome, and in Italy. They pretended that the issue lay between a rebellious proconsul and legitimate authority. Such venturesome expedients are commonly the work of hot blood and muddled heads. The error was double and damning. Disillusion followed swiftly. Even Cato was dismayed. It had confidently been expected that the solid and respectable classes in the towns of Italy would rally in defence of the authority of the Senate and the liberties of the Roman people, that all the land would rise as one man against the invader. Nothing of the kind happened. Italy was apathetic to the war-cry of the republic in danger, skeptical about its champions. The very virtues for which the propertied classes were sedulously praised by politicians at Rome forbade intervention in a struggle which was not their own. . . . Caesar, it is true, had only a legion to hand; the bulk of his army was still far away. But he swept down the eastern coast of Italy, gathering troops, momentum and confidence as he went. Within two months of the crossing of the Rubicon he was master of Italy. . . .

Yet, even so, until the legions joined battle on the plain of Pharsalus, the odds lay heavily against Caesar. Fortune, the devotion of his veteran legionaries, and the divided counsels of his adversaries secured the crowning victory. But three years more of fighting were needed to stamp out the last and bitter resistance of the Pompeian cause in Africa and in Spain. "They would have it thus," said Caesar as he gazed upon the Roman dead at Pharsalus, half in patriot grief for the havoc of civil war, half in impatience and resentment. They had cheated Caesar of the true glory of a Roman aristocrat—to contend with his peers for primacy, not to destroy them. His enemies had the laugh on him in death. . . . That was the nemesis of ambition and glory, to be thwarted in the end. After such wreckage, the task of rebuilding confronted him, stern and thankless. Without the sincere and patriotic co-operation of the governing class, the attempt would be all in vain, the mere creation of arbitrary power, doomed to perish in violence. It was rational to suspend judgment about the guilt of the civil war. Pompeius had been little better, if at all, than his younger and more active rival, a spurious and disquieting champion of legitimate authority when men recalled the earlier career and inordinate ambition of the Sullan partisan who had first defied and then destroyed the Senate's rule. Each had sought armed domination. Had Pompeius conquered in battle, the republic could hardly have survived. A few years, and Pompeius the dictator would have been assassinated in the Senate by honorable men at the foot of his own statue. . . . [Caesar] expressed alarming opinions about the republic—"it was only a name: Sulla, by resigning supreme power, showed that he was an ignorant fellow." Caesar postponed decision about the permanent ordering of the state. It was too difficult. Instead, he would set out for the wars again, to Macedonia and to the eastern frontier of the empire. At Rome he was hampered: abroad he might enjoy his conscious mastery of men and events as before in Gaul. Easy victories—but not the urgent needs of the Roman people. About Caesar's ultimate designs there can be opinion, but no certainty. . . .

Brutus and his allies might invoke philosophy or an ancestor who had liberated Rome. . . . Dubious history and irrelevant. The liberators knew what they were about. Honorable men grasped the assassin's dagger to slay a Roman aristocrat, a friend and a benefactor, for better reasons than that. They stood, not merely for the traditions and the institutions of the free state, but very precisely for the dignity and the interests of their own order. Liberty and the laws are high-sounding words. They will often be rendered, on a cool estimate, as privilege and vested interests.

It is not necessary to believe that Caesar planned to establish at Rome a "Hellenistic monarchy," whatever meaning may attach to that phrase. The dictatorship was enough. The rule of the nobles, he could see, was an anachronism in a world-empire; and so was the power of the Roman plebs when all Italy enjoyed the franchise. Caesar in truth was more conservative and Roman than many have fancied; and no Roman conceived of government save through an oligarchy. But Caesar was being forced into an autocratic position. It meant the lasting domination of one man instead of the rule of the law, the constitution and the Senate; it announced the triumph soon or late of new forces and new ideas, the elevation of the army and the provinces, the depression of the traditional governing class. Caesar's autocracy appeared to be much more than a temporary expedient to liquidate the heritage of the civil war and reinvigorate the organs of the Roman state. It was going to last—and the Roman aristocracy was not to be permitted to govern and exploit the empire in its own fashion. The tragedies of history do not arise from the conflict of conventional right and wrong. They are more august and more complex. Caesar and Brutus each had right on his side.

5

THE CONVERSION OF CONSTANTINE

The conversion of the Roman emperor Constantine to Christianity marked a turning point in the history of the church. Arising from obscure beginnings in the first century, Christianity was often at odds with the Roman state over the public worship of the state gods, which to Romans was a token act of loyalty but to Christians was idolatry. Sporadically the church felt the scourge of persecution, and rulers as varied as Nero and Marcus Aurelius believed that Christians were subversive enemies of society. The first empire-wide persecution began in 250 under the emperor Decius. Many Christians died for their faith, but some bowed to the will of the state, and others purchased false certificates of submission. In 260 the emperor Gallienus halted all persecutions, restored confiscated property to the bishops, and gave the church legal protection as a religion recognized by the state. Though still a minority in the empire, the number of Christians was considerable, and the sect had acquired the respectability of a hereditary religion. Apostolic simplicity had vanished long before—many Christians were affluent and worldly-wise, and a few were members of the ruling class. Some Christians embraced the un-Christlike profession of soldiering, and the bishops formed a highly able organizational elite. The Christian leadership did not hesitate to ask a pagan emperor, Aurelian, to unseat the bishop of Antioch on charges of heresy and misconduct. Stronger than ever, the church was able to withstand its last great trial, a severe persecution under Diocletian. The emperor himself had little enthusiasm for the persecution, but his younger colleague Galerius was a rabid bigot and produced an oracle from Apollo to justify the attack on Christianity. The persecution lasted from 303 to 311 when Galerius changed his policy and restored toleration. In the Eastern provinces, bigotry had reigned supreme, but in the West Galerius' colleague Constantius had done little more than close churches. In 313 Constantius' son Constantine and his colleague Licinius agreed on complete freedom of religion for their subjects. This policy—the miscalled Edict of Milan—was aimed at their rival in the East, Maximinus Daia, who had succeeded Galerius but revived a brief persecution. Not only had the Christians emerged intact from a long and bitter ordeal, but they now had a formidable champion, for one of the emperors, Constantine, had become their patron. In 324 Constantine was sole emperor, and the Christians were the favored religious faction in the Roman Empire. From Constantine on, all Roman emperors (save Julian) were Christians, and Christianity was the state religion by the end of the fourth century. The triumphant church promptly persecuted pagans and heretics.

The man responsible for the crucial shift in imperial religious policy was Constantine, an ambitious and battle-hardened politician who fought his way to supreme power through bloody civil wars. At the end of the third century, the emperor Diocletian had established a governmental system in which power was shared among four men at the highest executive level in the state. Diocletian and his colleague Maximian were senior emperors with the title of Augustus; Constantius and Galerius were junior emperors, or Caesars. After twenty years in power, the Augusti resigned and Constantius and Galerius moved up, appointing in turn new Caesars. Without the strong leadership of Diocletian, the system of collective rule collapsed in a power struggle between the new generation of rival Augusti—Constantine and Licinius against Maximinus Daia and Maximian's son Maxentius. Even old Maximian returned to politics long enough to back his son and then quarrel with him, turn to Constantine and quarrel again, and die in an abortive revolt against Constantine, who had married his daughter Fausta. In 312 Constantine defeated Maxentius at the battle of the Milvian bridge, and Licinius destroyed Daia the following year. For a decade the victors ruled as co-emperors, but Constantine and Licinius eventually fell out and Constantine alone survived. Though he secured absolute power in 324, the emperor was distressed by the Arian controversy which split the Christians of the East. In 325 Constantine convened an ecumenical council at Nicaea and influenced its decision against the beliefs of Arius. Personally, the emperor felt that the theologians were splitting hairs when they argued over the equality of God the Father and the Son. However, his authoritarian mind could tolerate no dissent, and he insisted that all churchmen subscribe to the vague Nicene creed. Beyond conformity in the interest of unity, Constantine asked nothing more, and some of his closest clerical friends were Arians. As he aged, the emperor grew obsessed with religion and spent great sums on churches and religious establishments. His mother Helena had followed his lead and become a Christian; in Palestine, the elderly lady discovered what she believed to be the cross on which Jesus had died. Constantine's piety was partly the result of an uneasy conscience, for he had executed his son Crispus on a false charge of attempted seduction made by the empress Fausta, whom the emperor later had steamed to death in her bath. In 337, knowing that he was dying, Constantine risked baptism and died in the odor of sanctity.

The date of Constantine's conversion to Christianity and the extent of his sincerity have been the subject of much scholarly debate. The ancient sources Lactantius and

Eusebius contradict each other, and Eusebius freely twisted history to glorify the church and its heroes. Even after he became a patron of Christianity in 312, the emperor did not cease using pagan devices, but this may be explained as political opportunism, since most of his subjects were pagans. The famous vision of a cross in the sky (if it happened) was not the only heavenly visitation in Constantine's life. In 310 Constantine had abandoned the cult of Hercules, the patron of his discredited father-in-law Maximian, and proclaimed his renewed devotion to Sol Invictus, the solar god of his father Constantius. Somewhere in Gaul, the ambitious Constantine glimpsed the sun god, according to a florid panegyrist:

. . . when you had turned aside to the most beautiful temple in the whole world, nay rather to a god present in actuality. For, O Constantine, you saw, I believe, your protector Apollo in company with Victory, offering you laurel crowns, each of which bears the presage of thirty years. . . . But why indeed do I say, "I believe"? You really saw the god and recognized yourself in the appearance of one to whom the prophecies of poets have declared that the rule of the whole world should belong.[1]

Did Constantine actually claim to have seen the solar deity together with the goddess Victoria? In the fourth century, such a hallucinatory episode is quite possible. As for Apollo, the sun god was the favorite deity of the armies and had been the official god of the empire, Sol Invictus, under Aurelian. Sol Invictus was also the patron deity of the family of Constantius, and Constantine's cross in the sky was close to the sun. In 312, in response to a dream, Constantine placed a symbol on his soldiers' shields and, later, on his own imperial standard—the letter X divided by a vertical line which looped to the right on top. To Christians, this was the Greek monogram of Christ (Chi Rho), but it could also be a solar symbol, for the overall impression is of a round and spoked figure. To the pagan soldier, the emblem was a sign of Sol Invictus, and the Senate at Rome attributed Constantine's victory at the Milvian bridge to "the god of heaven." However equivocal the emblem was, Constantine acknowledged the Christian god as the bestower of his victory, but in the beginning the emperor's notion of Christ was probably much like his view of Sol Invictus, another god of battle.

Few doubt that in 312 Constantine had a dream of the emblem, which later seemed so lucky in war, but an earlier daylight vision of a cross in the sky raises doubts. Eusebius insists that he received the story of the cross from the emperor himself under oath, but Constantine was an elderly priest-ridden man when he confided the miracle to the bishop. It is noteworthy that Constantine did not inform his son's Christian tutor, Lactantius, of the wonderful vision. Lactantius was not one to disparage miracles, but he was only told of the dream of the magic emblem. If he could see Apollo in Gaul, the emperor could surely imagine another vision in his pious old age. Since his father Constantius was tolerant toward Christianity, it is not unlikely that young Constantine had a vague interest in Christ though not to the exclusion of other gods before 312. In the third century, the emperor Severus Alexander had a statue of Jesus beside pagan saints in his private chapel, and the emperor

[1] Panegyrici Latini 6(7) 21.3–5, translated by J. Stevenson, A New Eusebius (London: Society for Promoting Christian Knowledge, 1960), p. 298.

Philip was so pro-Christian that some people claimed he was a member of the sect. After the victory of 312 Christ was Constantine's patron deity, and the emperor was consistently grateful for the rest of his life. However, Constantine was never a Roman equivalent of the saintly King Louis IX of France, and Julian the Apostate was a more truly religious man than his uncle Constantine ever was. Though he believed in the god who had given him victory and power, Constantine never embraced the moral regimen of Christianity and never considered the church superior to the authority of a Christian emperor. Surrounded by bishops and saturated with Christian propaganda, he took a great interest in ecclesiastical politics and policy making, but Constantine was no more Christlike than Henry VIII or the other despots whom history calls Christian.

The American historian Henry Adams made a useful, if sardonic, comment on the first Christian emperor:

Good taste forbids saying that Constantine the Great speculated as audaciously as a modern stockbroker on values of which he knew at the utmost only the volume; or that he merged all uncertain forces into a single trust which he enormously overcapitalized and forced on the market; but this is the substance of what Constantine himself said in his Edict of Milan in the year 313, which admitted Christianity into the Trust of State Religions. Regarded as an Act of Congress, it runs: "We have resolved to grant to Christians as well as all others the liberty to practice the religion they prefer, in order that whatever exists of divinity or celestial power may help and favor us and all who are under our government." The empire pursued power — not merely spiritual but physical — in the sense in which Constantine issued his army order the year before at the battle of the Milvian bridge: *In this sign conquer!* using the Cross as a train of artillery which, to his mind, it was. Society accepted it in the same character.[2]

In our present irreligious age, we often lose sight of what religion meant to men like Constantine: supernatural power, magic protection, and little ethical content. After his death, the Greek church canonized him as a saint, and the Roman Senate made him a god. However, Constantine did not really qualify for either distinction.

LACTANTIUS AND EUSEBIUS

CONSTANTINE: THE CHRISTIAN SOURCES

The contemporary Christian sources for the conversion of Constantine in 312 are Lactantius and Eusebius. A convert to Christianity, Lactantius was a professor of Latin rhetoric who had been employed by the emperor Diocletian and later became the tutor of Constantine's son, Crispus. A fervent and prolific apologist for the Christian faith, Lactantius wrote a bitter treatise, *How the Persecutors Died,* in which he described with great relish the unhappy deaths of emperors who had oppressed the church. Lactantius died about 320, and his account of the events of 312 is our earliest version. Eusebius of Caesarea was born a Christian and became a bishop.

[2] Henry Adams, *The Education of Henry Adams* (New York: The Modern Library, 1931), pp. 478–479.

Scholarly and enthusiastic, he was the first major historian of Christianity. He revised his *Ecclesiastical History* four times to conform to shifts in imperial policy; the final edition was published after Constantine had destroyed his colleague Licinius in 324 and before Constantine executed his own son Crispus in 326. Eusebius also wrote a florid *Life of Constantine* after the emperor's death in 337. A poor source, the biography of Constantine is exaggerated and inaccurate—it also contains the most sensational account of Constantine's conversion, which Eusebius admits would be unbelievable had he not heard it from the aged and pious emperor himself.

1. LACTANTIUS

A civil war broke out between Constantine and Maxentius. Although Maxentius kept himself within Rome because the soothsayers had foretold that if he went out of it he should perish, yet he conducted the military operations by able generals. In forces he exceeded his adversary, for he had not only his father's army . . . but also his own, which he had lately drawn together out of Mauretania and Italy. They fought and the troops of Maxentius prevailed. At length Constantine, with steady courage and a mind prepared for every event, led his whole forces to the neighborhood of Rome and encamped them opposite to the Milvian bridge. . . . Constantine was directed in a dream to cause the heavenly sign to be delineated on the shields of his soldiers, and so to proceed to battle. He did as he had been commanded, and he marked on their shields the letter X, with a perpendicular line drawn through it and turned round . . . at the top, being the cipher of Christ. Having this sign, his troops stood to arms. The enemies advanced, but without their emperor, and they crossed the bridge. The armies met and fought with the utmost exertions of valor and firmly maintained their ground. In the meantime a sedition arose at Rome, and Maxentius was reviled as one who had abandoned all concern for the safety of the commonweal, and suddenly, while he exhibited the Circensian games on the anniversary of his reign, the people cried with one voice, "Constantine cannot be overcome!" Dismayed at this, Maxentius burst from the assembly and, having called some senators together, ordered the Sibylline books to be searched. In them it was found that—"On the same day the enemy of the Romans should perish." Led by this response to the hopes of victory, he went to the field. The bridge in his rear was broken down. At sight of that, the battle grew hotter. The hand of the Lord prevailed, and the forces of Maxentius were routed. He fled towards the broken bridge, but the multitude pressing on him, he was driven headlong into the Tiber. This destructive war being ended, Constantine was acknowledged as emperor, with great rejoicings, by the Senate and people of Rome.

2. EUSEBIUS IN 325

Thus when Constantine . . . an emperor, born of an emperor, a pious son of a most pious and prudent father, and Licinius, second to him—two God-beloved emperors, honored alike for their intelligence and their piety—being stirred up against the two most impious tyrants [Maxentius and Maximinus Daia] by God . . . , engaged in formal war against them, with God as their ally, Maxentius was defeated at Rome by Constantine in a remarkable manner, and the tyrant of the East [Daia] did not long survive him but met a most shameful death at the hand of Licinius, who had not yet become insane. Constantine, who was the superior both in dignity and imperial rank, first took compassion upon those who were oppressed at Rome and, having invoked in prayer the God of heaven . . . and Jesus Christ himself as his aid, advanced with his whole army, proposing to restore to the Romans their ancestral liberty. But Maxentius, putting confidence rather in the arts of sorcery than in the devotion of his subjects, did not dare to go forth beyond the gates of the city but fortified every place and district and town which was enslaved by him, in the neighborhood of

From Lactantius, *How the Persecutors Died*, 44, tr. William Fletcher, in *The Ante-Nicene Fathers*, ed. Alexander Roberts (Buffalo: The Christian Literature Co. (1886), Vol. VII, p. 318. [This passage was written not long after 314. Editor's note.]

From Eusebius, *Ecclesiastical History*, IX, 9.1–12, tr. Arthur C. McGiffert, in *A Select Library of the Nicene and Post-Nicene Fathers*, ed. Philip Schaff (Grand Rapids, Mich., 1952), Vol. I, pp. 363–64. Reprinted by permission of Wm. B. Eerdmans Publishing Company.

Rome and in all Italy, with an immense multitude of troops and with innumerable bands of soldiers. But the emperor, relying upon the assistance of God, attacked the first, second, and third army of the tyrant and conquered them all; and having advanced through the greater part of Italy, was already very near Rome. Then, that he might not be compelled to wage war with the Romans for the sake of the tyrant, God himself drew the latter, as if bound in chains, some distance without the gates, and confirmed those threats against the impious which had been anciently inscribed in sacred books—disbelieved, indeed, by most as a myth, but believed by the faithful—confirmed them, in a word, by the deed itself to all, both believers and unbelievers, that saw the wonder with their eyes. . . . Maxentius . . . with his soldiers and body-guards "went down into the depths like a stone," when he fled before the power of God which was with Constantine and passed through the river which lay in his way, over which he had formed a bridge with boats, and thus prepared the means of his own destruction. . . . Then, the bridge over the river being broken, the passageway settled down and immediately the boats with the men disappeared in the depths, and that most impious one himself first of all. . . . Constantine . . . entered Rome in triumph. Immediately all the members of the Senate and the other most celebrated men with the whole Roman people, together with children and women, received him as their deliverer, their savior, and their benefactor, with shining eyes and with their whole souls, with shouts of gladness and unbounded joy. But he, as one possessed of inborn piety toward God, did not exult in the shouts, nor was he elated by the praises, but perceiving that his aid was from God, he immediately commanded that a trophy of the Savior's passion be put in the hand of his own statue. And when he had placed it, with the saving sign of the cross in its right hand, in the most public place in Rome, he commanded that the following inscription should be engraved upon it in the Roman tongue: "By this salutary sign, the true proof of bravery, I have saved and freed your city from the yoke of the tyrant; and moreover, having set at liberty both the Senate and the people of Rome, I have restored them to their ancient distinction and splendor." And after this both Constantine himself and with him the emperor Licinius, who had not yet been seized by that madness into which he later fell, . . . with one will and

mind drew up a full and most complete decree in behalf of the Christians.

3. EUSEBIUS AFTER 337

Being convinced . . . that he needed some more powerful aid than his military forces could afford him on account of the wicked and magical enchantments which were so diligently practiced by the tyrant, [Constantine] sought divine assistance, deeming the possession of arms and a numerous soldiery of secondary importance, but believing the cooperating power of Deity invincible and not to be shaken. He considered, therefore, on what god he might rely for protection and assistance. While engaged in this enquiry, the thought occurred to him, that, of the many emperors who had preceded him, those who had rested their hopes in a multitude of gods and served them with sacrifices and offerings, had in the first place been deceived by flattering predictions and oracles which promised them all prosperity, and at last had met with an unhappy end, while not one of their gods had stood by to warn them of the impending wrath of heaven; while one alone who had pursued an entirely opposite course, who had condemned their error, and honored the one supreme god during his whole life, had found him to be the savior and protector of his empire and the giver of every good thing. Reflecting on this and well weighing the fact that they who had trusted in many gods had also fallen by manifold forms of death without leaving behind them either family or offspring, stock, name, or memorial among men: while the god of his father had given to him, on the other hand, manifestations of his power and very many tokens: and considering further that those who had already taken arms against the tyrant and had marched to the battlefield under the protection of a multitude of gods, had met with a dishonorable end . . . , he judged it to be folly indeed to join in the idle worship of those who were no gods . . . and therefore felt it incumbent on him to honor his father's god alone. Accordingly he called on him with earnest prayer and supplications that he would reveal to him who he was and stretch forth his right hand to help him in his present difficulties. And while he was thus praying with fervent entreaty, a most marvelous sign appeared to him from heaven, the account of which

From Eusebius, *Life of Constantine*, I, 27–29, tr. Ernest C. Richardson, in *A Select Library of the Nicene and Post-Nicene Fathers*, ed. Philip Schaff (Grand Rapids, Mich., 1952), Vol. I, pp. 489–90. Reprinted by permission of Wm. B. Erdmans Publishing Company.

it might have been hard to believe had it been related by any other person. But since the victorious emperor himself long afterwards declared it to the writer of this history, when he was honored with his acquaintance and society, and confirmed his statement by an oath, who could hesitate to accredit the relation, especially since the testimony of after-time has established its truth? He said that about noon, when the day was already beginning to decline, he saw with his own eyes the trophy of a cross of light in the heavens above the sun and bearing the inscription, Conquer by This. At this sight he himself was struck with amazement, and his whole army also, which followed him on this expedition and witnessed the miracle. He said, moreover, that he doubted within himself what the import of this apparition could be. And while he continued to ponder and reason on its meaning, night suddenly came on; then in his sleep the Christ . . . appeared to him with the same sign which he had seen in the heavens and commanded him to make a likeness of that sign which he had seen in the heavens and to use it as a safeguard in all engagements with his enemies.

EDWARD GIBBON

CONSTANTINE: AN EIGHTEENTH-CENTURY VIEW

Edward Gibbon (1737–1794) was a pompous little man but a giant among historians, for it is generally agreed that his *History of the Decline and Fall of the Roman Empire* (6 volumes: 1776–1783) is the greatest historical work written in the English language. He saw history on a grand scale and composed a prose epic on the collapse of a world which he admired. Gibbon had vast learning, a sharp wit, and a rhythmic style. Out of a welter of chaotic sources he made a coherent whole, and his account of Rome down to the fall of the Western empire is still worth the attention of scholars. However, Gibbon's view of Imperial Rome was warped by his Tory political bias and his thorough dislike of Christianity. Born an Anglican, he became a Roman Catholic as a youth, but his father soon sent him to a Calvinist minister in Switzerland to cure the boy of "Papism." After a thorough exposure to theological disputes and church history, Gibbon acquired a horror of organizational Christianity and became a skeptical deist. Such an attitude was useful when Gibbon tackled the problem of Constantine, who was regarded by most people as a plaster saint. Though indebted to the work of ecclesiastical historians, Gibbon was a man of the Enlightenment and pounced with glee on the threadbare image of Constantine.

In the consideration of a subject which may be examined with impartiality but cannot be viewed with indifference, a difficulty immediately arises of a very unexpected nature—that of ascertaining the real and precise date of the conversion of Constantine. . . . The learned Eusebius has ascribed the faith of Constantine to the miraculous sign which was displayed in the heavens whilst he meditated and prepared the Italian expedition. The historian Zosimus maliciously asserts that the emperor had imbrued his hands in the blood of his eldest son before he publicly renounced the gods of Rome and of his ancestors. The perplexity produced by these discordant authorities is derived from the behavior of Constantine himself. According to the strictness of ecclesiastical language, the first of the Christian emperors was un-

From *The Decline and Fall of the Roman Empire* (Vol. I) by Edward Gibbon. Everyman's Edition, pp. 634–36, 646–51, 653–54. Reprinted by permission of E. P. Dutton & Co., Inc., and J. M. Dent & Sons Ltd.

worthy of that name till the moment of his death, since it was only during his last illness that he . . . was admitted by the initiatory rites of baptism into the number of the faithful. The Christianity of Constantine must be allowed in a much more vague and qualified sense; and the nicest accuracy is required in tracing the slow and almost imperceptible gradations by which the monarch declared himself the protector and at length the proselyte of the church. . . .

[Lactantius[1]] affirms with the most perfect confidence that in the night which preceded the last battle against Maxentius, Constantine was admonished in a dream to inscribe the shields of his soldiers with the *celestial sign of God*, the sacred monogram of the name of Christ; that he executed the commands of Heaven, and that his valor and obedience were rewarded by the decisive victory of the Milvian Bridge. Some considerations might perhaps incline a skeptical mind to suspect the judgment or the veracity of the rhetorician whose pen, either from zeal or interest, was devoted to the cause of the prevailing faction. He appears to have published his *Deaths of the Persecutors* at Nicomedia about three years after the Roman victory; but the interval of a thousand miles and a thousand days will allow an ample latitude for the invention of declaimers, the credulity of party, and the tacit approbation of the emperor himself, who might listen without indignation to a marvellous tale which exalted his fame and promoted his designs. In favor of Licinius, who still dissembled his animosity to the Christians, the same author has provided a similar vision of a form of prayer, which was communicated by an angel, and repeated by the whole army before they engaged the legions of the tyrant [Daia]. The frequent repetition of miracles serves to provoke, where it does not subdue, the reason of mankind; but if the dream of Constantine be separately considered, it may be naturally explained either by the policy or the enthusiasm of the emperor. Whilst his anxiety for the approaching day which must decide the fate of the empire was suspended by a short and interrupted slumber, the venerable form of Christ and the well-known symbol of his religion might forcibly offer themselves to the active fancy of a prince who reverenced the name, and had perhaps secretly implored the power, of the god of the Christians. . . .

The Christian fable of Eusebius, which in the space

[1] Gibbon did not believe that Lactantius wrote the tract on the deaths of the persecutors, but most modern scholars do. The point does not impair Gibbon's thesis. [Editor's note.]

of twenty-six years might arise from the original dream, is cast in an . . . elegant mold. In one of the marches of Constantine he is reported to have seen with his own eyes the luminous trophy of the cross placed above the meridian sun and inscribed with the following words: By This Conquer. This amazing object in the sky astonished the whole army as well as the emperor himself who was yet undetermined in the choice of a religion: but his astonishment was converted into faith by the vision of the ensuing night. Christ appeared before his eyes and displaying the same celestial sign of the cross, he directed Constantine to frame a similar standard and to march with an assurance of victory against Maxentius and all his enemies. The learned bishop of Caesarea appears to be sensible that the recent discovery of this marvellous anecdote would excite some surprise and distrust among the most pious of his readers. Yet, instead of ascertaining the precise circumstances of time and place, which always serve to detect falsehood or establish truth; instead of collecting and recording the evidence of so many living witnesses who must have been spectators of this stupendous miracle, Eusebius contents himself with alleging a very singular testimony, that of the deceased Constantine, who many years after the event in the freedom of conversation had related to him this extraordinary incident of his own life and had attested the truth of it by a solemn oath. The prudence and gratitude of the learned prelate forbade him to suspect the veracity of his victorious master, but he plainly intimates that, in a fact of such a nature, he should have refused his assent to any meaner authority. This motive of credibility could not survive the power of the Flavian family, and the celestial sign . . . was disregarded by the Christians of the age which immediately followed the conversion of Constantine. . . .

The protestant and philosophic readers of the present age will incline to believe that, in the account of his own conversion, Constantine attested a wilful falsehood by a solemn and deliberate perjury. They may not hesitate to pronounce that in the choice of a religion his mind was determined only by a sense of interest, and that . . . he used the altars of the church as a convenient footstool to the throne of the empire. A conclusion so harsh and so absolute is not, however, warranted by our knowledge of human nature, of Constantine, or of Christianity. In an age of religious fervor the most artful statesmen are observed to feel some part of the enthusiasm which they inspire, and the most orthodox saints assume the dangerous privilege of defending the cause of truth by the arms of deceit and falsehood. Personal interest is often the standard of our belief as well as of our practice, and the same motives of temporal advantage which might influence the public conduct and professions of Constantine would insensibly dispose his mind to embrace a religion so propitious to his fame and fortunes. His vanity was gratified by the flattering assurance that *he* had been chosen by Heaven to reign over the earth; success had justified his divine title to the throne, and that title was founded on the truth of the Christian revelation. As real virtue is sometimes excited by undeserved applause, the specious piety of Constantine, if at first it was only specious, might gradually by the influence of praise, of habit, and of example be matured into serious faith and fervent devotion. The bishops and teachers of the new sect, whose dress and manners had not qualified them for the residence of a court, were admitted to the imperial table. . . . Lactantius, who has adorned the precepts of the Gospel with the eloquence of Cicero, and Eusebius, who has consecrated the learning and philosophy of the Greeks to the service of religion, were both received into the friendship and familiarity of their sovereign; and those able masters of controversy could patiently watch the soft and yielding moments of persuasion and dexterously apply the arguments which were the best adapted to his character and understanding. Whatever advantages might be derived from the acquisition of an imperial proselyte, he was distinguished by the splendor of his purple, rather than by the superiority of wisdom or virtue, from the many thousands of his subjects who had embraced the doctrines of Christianity. Nor can it be deemed incredible that the mind of an unlettered soldier should have yielded to the weight of evidence which, in a more enlightened age, has satis-fied or subdued the reason of a Grotius, a Pascal, or a Locke. . . .

The sublime theory of the Gospel had made a much fainter impression on the heart than on the understanding of Constantine. . . . He pursued the great object of his ambition through the dark and bloody paths of war and policy; and after the victory he abandoned himself without moderation to the abuse of his fortune. Instead of asserting his just superiority above the imperfect heroism and profane philosophy of Trajan and the Antonines, the mature age of Constantine forfeited the reputation which he had acquired in his youth. As he gradually advanced in the knowledge of truth, he proportionably declined in the practice of virtue; and the same year of his reign in which he convened the council of Nicaea was polluted by the execution, or rather murder, of his eldest son. . . . At the time of the death of Crispus the emperor could no longer hesitate in the choice of a religion; he could no longer be ignorant that the church was possessed of an infallible remedy, though he chose to defer the application of it till the approach of death had removed the temptation and danger of a relapse. The bishops whom he summoned in his last illness to the palace of Nicomedia were edified by the fervor with which he requested and received the sacrament of baptism, by the solemn protestation that the remainder of his life should be worthy of a disciple of Christ, and by his humble refusal to wear the imperial purple after he had been clothed in the white garment of a neophyte. The example and reputation of Constantine seemed to countenance the delay of baptism. Future tyrants were encouraged to believe that the innocent blood which they might shed in a long reign would instantly be washed away in the waters of regeneration. . . .

JAKOB BURCKHARDT

CONSTANTINE: "THE EGOIST ROBED IN PURPLE"

The Swiss writer Jakob Burckhardt (1818–1897) was a renowned cultural historian and art critic. His stimulating study of *The Civilization of the Renaissance in Italy* (1860) was extremely influential and gave rise to the image of the "Renaissance Man." *The Age of Constantine the Great* (1852) is less well-known but is also characterized by Burckhardt's wide learning and an overactive historical imagination.

Like his friend Nietzsche, Burckhardt disliked the nineteenth century with its crass materialism, bourgeois hypocrisy, and love of power and success. His books are less histories than extended historical essays, crammed with insights and biases. A man of great sensitivity, Burckhardt believed that the past could be recaptured through informed intuition. His intuition told him that Gibbon had been too soft on Constantine.

Constantine's historical memory has suffered the greatest misfortune conceivable. . . . He has fallen into the hands of the most objectionable of all eulogists, who has utterly falsified his likeness. The man is Eusebius of Caesarea and the book his *Life of Constantine*. The man who with all his faults was always significant and always powerful is here presented in the guise of a sanctimonious devotee; in point of fact his numerous misdeeds are amply documented in a number of passages. Eusebius' equivocal praise is basically insincere. He speaks of the man but really means a cause, and that cause is the hierarchy, so strongly and richly established by Constantine. . . . Virtually throughout his life Constantine never assumed the guise of or gave himself out as a Christian but kept his free personal convictions quite unconcealed to his very last days. That Eusebius is fully capable of ignoring and concealing such a fact he himself reveals by his earlier characterization of Licinius, whom he claims straightway as a Christian emperor beloved of God as long as the war against Maximinus Daia is involved, though he must have known that Licinius was nothing else than a tolerant pagan. It is highly probable that his treatment of Constantine is of a similar character. [If this is true,] the odious hypocrisy which disfigures his character would disappear, and we should have instead a calculating politician who shrewdly employed all available physical resources and spiritual powers to the one end of maintaining himself and his rule without surrendering himself wholly to any party. It is true that the picture of such an egoist is not very edifying either, but history has had ample opportunity to grow accustomed to his like. . . .

Eusebius is no fanatic; he understands Constantine's secular spirit and his cold and terrible lust for power well enough and doubtless knows the true causes of the war [with Licinius] quite precisely. But he is the first thoroughly dishonest historian of antiquity. His tactic, which enjoyed a brilliant success in his own day and throughout the Middle Ages, consisted in making the first great protector of the church at all costs an ideal of humanity according to his lights and above all an ideal for future rulers. Hence we have lost the picture of a genius in stature who knew no moral scruple in politics and regarded the religious question exclusively from the point of view of political expediency. . . . He found it advisable to attach himself more closely to the Christians after this war, and . . . the elevation of Christianity to the position of state religion was thus consummated. But Constantine was a more honorable man than Eusebius; he rather allowed these events to transpire than intervened actively on their behalf, and as regards his own personal conviction, he enjoined definite beliefs upon his subjects as little as did Napoleon in his concordat. To pass for a Christian would, indeed, have been a great presumption on his part. Not long after the council of Nicaea he suddenly had Crispus, his excellent son by his first marriage and a pupil of Lactantius, put to death . . . and soon thereafter he had his wife Fausta . . . drowned in her bath. . . .

Attempts have often been made to penetrate into the religious consciousness of Constantine and to construct a hypothetical picture of changes in his religious convictions. Such efforts are futile. In a genius driven without surcease by ambition and lust for power, there can be no question of Christianity and paganism, of conscious religiosity or irreligiosity; such a man is essentially unreligious, even if he pictures himself standing in the midst of a churchly community. Holiness he understands only as a reminiscence or as a superstitious vagary. Moments of inward reflection, which for a religious man are in the nature of worship, he consumes in a different sort of fire. World-embracing plans and mighty dreams lead him by an easy road to the streams of blood of slaughtered armies. He thinks that he will be at peace when he has achieved this or the other goal, whatever it may be that is wanting to make his possessions complete. But in the meantime all of his energies, spiritual as well as physical, are devoted to the great goal of dominion, and if he ever pauses to think of his convictions, he finds they are pure fatalism. . . .

After the war with Maxentius . . . Constantine not only permitted the toleration of Christianity as a lawful religion, but spread abroad in the army an emblem which every man could interpret as he pleased but which the Christians would refer to themselves. The interlocked letters X and P, which form the beginning of the word Christ . . . , were introduced on the shields of the soldiers, we are told, even before the war. At the same time or later the same emblem, surrounded by gold and jewels, was attached to a large battle standard [*labarum*]. . . . The emblem even had its own tent into which the emperor mysteriously retired before any important affair. Should not all this signify an open profession? First of all it is to be noticed that Constantine employed this sign not among the populace but in the army. . . . Among the Gauls and Britons in the army there were certainly many Christians and indifferent pagans, and to the Germans the religion of their leader was a matter of no consequence. On his part it was an experiment that obliged him to nothing more than toleration, which was already in fact the rule in his previous domains and which he now extended to his conquests also. For him Christ may have rated as a god along with other gods, and the professors of Christ's religion along with the servants of the pagan deities. We shall not deny the possibility that Constantine developed a kind of superstition in favor of Christ, and that he may even have brought that name into some kind of confused relationship with the sun-god. But without doubt he was concerned exclusively with success; if he had met with a powerful resistance against XP in Italy, the symbol would quickly have disappeared from shields and standards. . . .

As soon as his lucid, empiric logic informed him that the Christians were good subjects, that they were numerous, and that the persecution could no longer have meaning in a reasonably governed state, his decision was taken. From the political point of view, the practical execution of his decision is wholly admirable. In his victorious hands the *labarum* was a physical representation at once of rule, of warlike power, and of the new religion.

The *esprit de corps* of his army, which had been victorious over one of the greatest armies of ancient history, hallowed the new symbol with the aura of the irresistible.

But the familiar miracle which Eusebius and those who copy him represent as taking place on the march against Maxentius must finally be eliminated from the pages of history. It has not even the value of a myth, indeed is not of popular origin, but was told to Eusebius by Constantine long afterwards and by Eusebius written up with intentionally vague bombast. The emperor indeed swore a great oath to the bishop that the thing was not imagined, but that he actually saw in heaven the cross with the inscription "In this sign thou shalt conquer," and that Christ actually appeared to him in a dream, and the rest; but history cannot take an oath of Constantine the Great too seriously, because among other things, he had his brother-in-law [Licinius] murdered despite assurances given under oath. Nor is Eusebius beyond having himself invented two-thirds of the story.

A great inconsistency in Constantine's outward bearing persists; he accepts the monogram of Christ as the emblem of his army and has the name of Jupiter on his triumphal arch erased, but at the same time he retains the old gods on his coins and especially the sun-god as his unconquerable companion, and on important occasions his outward conduct is entirely pagan. This cleavage rather increases than decreases in his latter years. But he wished to give direct guarantees to both religions, and he was powerful enough to maintain a twofold position. . . . A glimmer of edification still clings to Constantine because so many admirable Christians of all centuries have claimed him for their own. But this last glimmer must also vanish. The Christian church has nothing to lose in this terrible though politically grandiose figure, just as paganism would have had nothing to gain by him. . . .

Let us now turn from the egoist robed in purple who measures and calculates all that he does or suffers to be done by the aggrandisement of his own power. Contrasted with this essentially frivolous authority of the state is the great and selfless devotion of many who gave away all of their possessions during their lifetime in order to "dedicate themselves to God."

FERDINAND LOT

CONSTANTINE: "AN ACT OF SUPERSTITION"

Ferdinand Lot (1866–1952) of the Sorbonne was one of the great medieval scholars of recent years. He wrote extensively and his *End of the Ancient World and the Beginnings of the Middle Ages* (1926) is a classic study of a vitally important period of transition. With urbanity and vast learning, Lot made a lasting contribution to the study of history, and his view of Constantine is a useful antidote to Burckhardt's total condemnation.

The edict [of toleration in 313] is no proof at all that Constantine passed over to Christianity. Was he even ever a Christian? This has been denied. Apart from Christian apologists, historians agree in seeing the founder of the Christian empire as a shrewd statesman, at bottom a religious skeptic, or at most a deist. They bring together all the points which show that up to his final victory over Licinius, Constantine kept the balance between paganism and Christianity. The Christian symbols to which Christian apologetics appeal they match with others which are definitely pagan. If the coins from a certain date onwards bear the Christian monogram, we read on the reverse "soli invicto comiti," an invocation to the sun-god, the god of the emperors and of the army since Claudius II and Aurelian . . ., the god also of Constantine himself in his youth. If the emperor grants privileges to the Christian churches, he does the same for the temples. He does not give up his purely pagan title of Pontifex Maximus. He entrusts the public offices to pagans as well as to Christians. At court, he is surrounded by philosophers and rhetoricians who naturally were pagans. He closed down the temples, it will be objected, but two or three only . . . which had become houses of ill fame. He prohibited sacrifices even in the home, but that was because he wished to bring everything into the light and under his control. Even after 324, after he had become a Christian "as far as he could be," he was still careful in his attitude to paganism. At most he defended Christianity and became a Christian at the end of his life, because he felt in this religion a "force which he did not wish to leave outside the grasp of his government." He seized the already fully established power of the episcopate. He realized what unique functionaries he would gain for his service by attracting to himself the bishops. Constantine resembles Bonaparte signing the concordat to reconcile the revolution and the church and to turn the bishops into more submissive prefects. "Supreme pagan pontiff by right, he would easily be the real head of Christendom and would thus rule over men's souls as well as over their bodies."

These interpretations of Constantine's thought are ingenious and probable. But they may also be entirely erroneous. There is a mania for crediting great men of the past with deep laid political schemes the idea of which perhaps never occurred to them. We forget that they may have been visionaries, and in that case the motives which they obeyed are of so special a kind that every psychological reconstruction based on political sense is bound to come to grief. In the first place, to think of Constantine as a disillusioned skeptic is more than arbitrary. There were no freethinkers at this time. All men from the lowest to the highest social stratum were religious or at least superstitious, even Diocletian, even Marcus Aurelius. Constantine when pagan was necessarily religious, Constantine when Christian was most certainly so. We see him concerned as to the problems of Christ's essential nature and his relation to the Father. He endeavored to restore unity to the church. Had he been indifferent, he would calmly have suffered the followers of Athanasius and of Arius to excommunicate each other and to set church against church, confining himself to maintaining the public peace and preventing the disciples of Jesus from killing each other. Doubtless

From Ferdinand Lot, *The End of the Ancient World and the Beginnings of the Middle Ages*, tr. Philip and Mariette Leon (New York, 1953), pp. 29–35, 37, 39. Reprinted by permission of Barnes & Noble, Inc., and Routledge & Kegan Paul Ltd.

he would have done better to adopt this attitude. But he intervened, and if he did so, it was because he believed in Truth, in the Absolute. In his adherence to Christianity sincerity played a part, and that part must have been great.

If we hold that he adhered to Christianity from policy we must believe that he had some interest in doing so. But what was this interest? A sovereign like Henry IV [of France], absolutely unable to bring over to his own faith subjects the majority of whom profess a doctrine different from his, may think it necessary to abandon his individual sentiments in order to bring about that unity of belief he deems indispensable for the good functioning of society. In that case, Constantine, even if he had been Christian at heart, would have been obliged to turn pagan. In spite of its marvellous power of expansion during the first three centuries of its existence, Christianity was far from having conquered the majority of the inhabitants of the Roman world. . . . The country in which Constantine was born and which had been ruled by his father and until 312 by himself, counts amongst the least Christian in the empire. It is a paradox that the emperor Constantine, a Westerner, should have imposed a religion which was widespread only in the oriental provinces of the empire. If there was any emperor to whose interest it was to embrace Christianity, it was Galerius and Maximinus Daia, but these on the contrary were its worst enemies. To go over to Christianity was, for a sovereign who reigned in the West, an act of sheer folly politically. It was even dangerous, for the army, the only real force in the state, was wholly pagan, addicted above all to the worship of the sun, and was destined for a long time to remain so. It being proved that Constantine had everything to lose and apparently nothing to gain by embracing Christianity, there is only one possible conclusion, namely that he yielded to a sudden impulse, which we may call one of a pathological or supernatural order as we prefer. He staked his fortune on the god of the Christians. Men's minds were troubled by the tragic fate of all those who had persecuted the Christians. Galerius himself, their fiercest adversary, had just done public penance and was asking his victims to pray for his salvation.[1] At Rome, Maxentius, who had the more numerous army, had invoked by incanta-

[1] Not really. In his final illness in 311, Galerius halted the persecution on the grounds that the Christians were too obstinate to be converted to "proper" piety. In return for this clemency, he asked them as loyal Romans to pray for his health and the welfare of the state. [Editor's note.]

tions all the powers of the pagan world, infernal and supernal, and his magic practices disturbed men's imaginations. For Constantine there was left the possibility of trying his luck by making an appeal to the new god, the god of the Christians. His conversion was an act of superstition.

But was he really converted? This brings us back to the question already raised. If by conversion is understood an inner moral reformation, the answer will no doubt be in the negative. But that is not the point at issue. The point is whether the emperor, after his victory over Maxentius, gave any external official signs of his adherence to the new faith. These signs are indisputable. At the moment of engaging in battle with his rival Maxentius, Constantine was not content with a mental prayer to the god of the Christians but had the symbol [XP] engraved on his soldiers' shields. But to make use of this talisman was to enter on an irrevocable compact with the deity who granted victory. After that it was impossible to draw back without risking the wrath of heaven. On the day after the victory . . . he allowed the wholly pagan Senate to offer him a statue as a symbol of his divinity, but he had a cross put in its hand. . . . He constantly intervenes in the affairs of the church; for example, in the quarrel between the Catholics and the Donatists in Africa on the very day after his triumph over Maxentius. He calls together the council of Nicaea . . . the holding of which coincides with his [twentieth year as emperor]. Only twenty years separate this ceremony from Diocletian's triumph at Rome, and yet an abyss yawns between these two dates. He undertakes propaganda. He invites his subjects to become converted to Christianity; he distributes presents of gold and silver pieces with Christian designs. He will write to his Persian rival Sapor to beg him to protect the Christians and to induce him to become a Christian himself. He becomes aggressive. He condemns the worship of Apollo whose oracle had let loose the persecution of Diocletian. . . . He upbraids his soldiers for sacrificing to Jupiter Capitolinus and brings upon himself the scorn of the Senate and the Roman people who had in large majority remained pagan. He forbids (after 330) functionaries to offer sacrifices to the gods in official ceremonies. . . . It is true also that he received baptism only on his deathbed. . . . But in the fourth century it was far from unusual not to ask for baptism until reaching adult age. Performed in extremis, it was considered a sure means to eternal salvation.

But the most striking manifestation of the emperor's sentiments is the foundation of Constantinople. . . . Having triumphed in a battle in which his rival [Licinius] put himself into his hands, Constantine owed the god of victories a striking sign of his gratitude. He showed the latter by transporting his capital from that Rome which was infected with an incurable paganism to a new city which was wholly Christian. . . . Constantine's conversion is the most important fact in the history of the Mediterranean world between the establishment of the hegemony of Rome and the setting up of Islam. To it is due the triumph of Christianity, which by transforming human psychology has dug an abyss between us and antiquity. Since the adoption of Christianity we have been living on a different plane.

NORMAN H. BAYNES

CONSTANTINE: A RECENT VIEW

Norman H. Baynes (1877–1961) of the University of London was a recognized authority on Byzantine history. His view of the conversion of Constantine was presented in the Raleigh Lecture on History in 1930.[1] The following passage is from the final chapter in the *Cambridge Ancient History* (12 volumes, 1922–1939), a monumental work of collective scholarship which is dated in parts but still indispensable for all students of ancient history.

Pope Marcellus, elected in 307, who was a rigorist, was opposed by a party which championed a more liberal treatment of [Christians who had renounced their faith during the recent persecution], and the two sections of the church met in bloody conflicts in the streets of the capital. In defence of public order Marcellus was banished by Maxentius. On April 8, 308 Maxentius permitted the election of Pope Eusebius, but he, too, met with opposition and was banished to Sicily. On July 2, 311 Miltiades was consecrated as bishop, and now Maxentius went farther than Galerius had done in his edict of toleration issued in the spring of the same year and restored to the church the property which had been confiscated during the persecution. It is important to realize that Maxentius in banishing two bishops was but doing his duty in maintaining order within the city. When Constantine marched upon Rome it was not to free the Christians from religious persecution.

Constantine as Caesar naturally continued to acknowledge Hercules as his official patron,

especially when . . . Constantine married Fausta, Maximian's daughter, and received from his father-in-law the title of Augustus. But with the treachery and death of Maximian in A.D. 310, a Herculian title to imperial power became impossible: some new basis must be found for Constantine's authority. Thus the panegyrist forthwith explains, what had not been realized previously, that Constantine was connected with the family of the heroic third-century emperor Claudius Gothicus. What the precise relationship may have been the orator discreetly does not seek to determine: the essential point to bring home to his hearers was that the derivation of Constantine's title from the grant of the discredited Maximian was nothing but an error. Already there had been two emperors in his family; Constantine was *born* an emperor. He alone of all his colleagues was one of a dynastic line. The fiction prevailed: the dynasty of the Second Flavians was securely founded. With the change in the title to the throne was associated a change in the emperor's religious allegiance. He now returns to the sun-worship of his Balkan ancestors, and henceforth Sol Invictus—Apollo—becomes his divine patron. Constantine's Herculian past is buried. This has been

[1] Norman H. Baynes, "Constantine and the Christian Church," *Proceedings of the British Academy*, Vol. XV (1929), pp. 341–42.

From Norman H. Baynes in *The Cambridge Ancient History* (Cambridge, Eng., 1939), Vol. XII. pp. 679–85; 698–99. Reprinted by permission of the Cambridge University Press.

called Constantine's first conversion. The new imperial faith is duly celebrated in the panegyric delivered at Trèves after the death of Maximian. The orator gives free rein to his fancy and imagines the appearance to the emperor of Apollo in his temple to which Constantine has made his pilgrimage. . . . No small importance has been attached to this vision by some scholars: it has been interpreted as the model on which the later Christian vision was fashioned. This is to do too much honor to the panegyrist's invention. . . .

As Licinius becomes the ally of Constantine, so Maxentius and [Daia] are drawn together. The revolt in Africa suppressed, his corn supplies secured, Maxentius can shelter behind the walls of [Rome]. . . . In 312 Constantine . . . decided to march against the "tyrant" who held the Western capital. There follows the lightning campaign which ended at the Milvian Bridge. From Gaul Constantine struck across the Alps: he left behind him troops to guard the frontier of the Rhine, and though we can form no precise numerical estimate of the strength of the army of invasion, it was less than 40,000 men. Maxentius, we are told, had in Italy some 100,000 soldiers, though many of these remained with the "tyrant" in Rome. . . . Constantine's great fear was that Maxentius would not quit Rome. It was the guardians of the Sibylline books who achieved for Constantine that which he himself would have been powerless to enforce. Maxentius determined to leave to his generals the command of his forces. . . . In the first encounter the soldiers of Maxentius were victorious. Then "Constantine moved all his forces nearer to the city and encamped in the neighborhood . . . of the Milvian Bridge." The real difficulty of the battle, if we accept this statement of Lactantius, is to understand how it was that, in face of the superior numbers of Maxentius, Constantine was allowed to execute this flanking movement unmolested. Are we to understand a previous retreat and a wide detour? Just before dawn on October 28 "Constantine was sleeping when he was bidden to mark . . . on the shields of his men the sublime sign of God and thus engage the enemy. He did as he was bidden and marked on the shields the letter X with a line drawn through it and turned round at the top, i.e. Christus." Maxentius on the same day, . . . ordered that the Sibylline books should be consulted: the answer was given that on that day the enemy of the Romans would perish. The battle was already begun when Maxentius, assured

of victory, joined his army. Constantine with like confidence threw his cavalry against the enemy, and his infantry followed. It was a bitterly contested struggle, but when the lines of Maxentius broke they could not retreat, for the Tiber ran close behind them. The bridge of boats by which they had crossed gave way under the press, and Maxentius perished with the fugitives.

Constantine as victor entered the Western capital. Against the advice of the augurs, in despite of his military counsellors, unsupported by the troops of Licinius, with incredible audacity Constantine had risked everything on a single hazard—and won. How shall that success be explained? Constantine himself knew well the reason for his victory: it had been won "by divine instigation," by a "courage" which was no mere human valor, but was a mysterious force which had its origin in God. And as the ground of that conviction tradition has repeated the story of the Vision of the Cross athwart the afternoon sun—a vision which came to Constantine, it seems, while he was still in Gaul before he began his march into Italy. For that Vision of the Cross we have no contemporary evidence: indeed our only evidence is the assertion of Eusebius, made after Constantine's death in the *Life of Constantine*, that the emperor had on his oath assured him of the fact. No mention of that vision occurs in any of the editions of the *Church History* of Eusebius: this of course proves nothing: Eusebius did not come into close contact with Constantine until A.D. 325, which is the probable date of the last edition of his *History*. It has been contended that the whole account is an interpolation of the Theodosian period, but that contention is at present unproven. In the year 351 Constantius [II] was granted a vision of the Cross in the heavens and it was then remarked that the son was more blessed than the father: Constantine had but found in the earth the true Cross: Constantius had seen it in the sky. Does this denote ignorance of the story of Eusebius or a politic denial of Eusebius' statement? Who shall say? The one thing which is critically illegitimate is to treat the account given by Lactantius of the dream of Constantine before the walls of Rome as though it described the same vision as that related by Eusebius. In recent discussions the two quite distinct divine interventions have at times been confused. But even though at present the historical student may be forced to conclude any discussion of the Eusebian report with a judgment of "not proven or disproven," to the present writer it appears that the account of the church historian is at least a true reflection of the emperor's own thought—or at least of his afterthought. Victory had been promised him by the god of the Christians: he had challenged the Christian god to an Ordeal by Battle and that god had kept his pledge. This belief of Constantine remains of fundamental significance for the understanding of the policy of the reign. . . .

The solar imagery of an earlier religious conviction is retained because Constantine is a member of a dynasty, and that solar imagery has become a part of a dynastic heraldry which proclaims an inherited title to imperial power. The student must therefore be prepared to recognize a conscious ambiguity in the acts of Constantine—an ambiguity necessarily arising from the ambiguous position of a Christian emperor ruling a pagan empire and bound to a pagan past. . . . In any attempt to recover and interpret the thought of Constantine, it must never be forgotten that he is a Roman emperor and a statesman. The emperor's ecclesiastical policy is a part of his imperial statesmanship, for that statesmanship was based upon the conviction of a mission in the service of the Christian god. Thus Christian theology may become a danger if it threatens to create disunion amongst the faithful. The dispute between Arius and his bishop is for Constantine an idle enquiry on points of the smallest consequence. Other Christian rulers have shared his outlook. We are reminded of the contempt of Elizabeth of England for the disputes of the German Protestants concerning the omnipresence of the body of Christ: to the Queen these were "unprofitable discussions." . . . Constantine's refusal to enquire curiously how bishops might interpret the creed of Nicaea provided only that they accepted it recalls Elizabeth's denial that she sought "to make a window into men's souls." . . . [In many respects Constantine followed in the footsteps of his pagan predecessors, but] there is none the less at this time a break and a turning-point in Roman history; the first Christian emperor was, indeed, as [the historian] Ammianus described him, . . . a revolutionary. Constantine sitting amongst the Christian bishops at the ecumenical council of Nicaea is in his own person the beginning of Europe's Middle Age.

1234567890

Constantine: A Recent View